SOLUTION 247-261

SOLUTION 247-261
LOVE

INGO NIERMANN (ED.)

SERIES EDITED BY INGO NIERMANN
STERNBERG PRESS

Preface:
The Imperative to Love

To love means that merely thinking of something gives pleasure. The discrepancy between the enjoyment of only envisioning something and the greater enjoyment of perceiving it with all senses, as well as the certainty that such perception will continue to be possible in the future, is what causes lovesickness. The lover often stipulates that he be permitted such comprehensive perception because his love is requited, and not just for the prospect of extraneous benefits such as food and money. An even more demanding lover not only wants to be loved in return: that love is also supposed to be exclusive. The other should not—or at least not with even remotely equal intensity—love anything as he loves the lover, and shouldn't permit anyone else the same comprehensive perception of himself. Such perception notably includes stimulation and being stimulated, but also encompasses comparatively minor acts such as the exhibition of the body and casual physical contact through fabric enveloping it.

Beyond the great apes and man's domesticated animals, outward signs of love are scarce. Other animals exchange few if any kisses and caresses; they also have sex fairly rarely. They may do it many times in a row, but each act is very brief, and sex is limited to days when the female is able to conceive. Humans and bonobos are the only animals that practice French kissing, oral sex, and face-to-face sex, and the only species whose females are horny when not ovulating. Sex and sexual love have a function that goes beyond procreation: they establish community ties. In all other animals, homosexuality is the only form of sexuality that doesn't directly serve reproduction.

Humans and their domestic animals even love each other across the species barrier: humans provide other animals with food and take them for walks and to the doctor to ensure their well-being just so they can have them around and fondle them and perhaps be loved by them as well. They've bred animals that are far better at looking at them with complete trust than any human. Who knows whether the cat begging to be let in and fed emulates the crying of children or, conversely, the crying child imitates the cats.

Although they have legs, domestic animals and children are safe objects of love because they can't escape the care of those who got or begot them without having to fear for their survival. Society stigmatizes sexual love of both—domestic animals and children—as exploitative and sick. The asexual paternalism it favors forms the template also for the charitable love of one's adult neighbors, self-dependent animals, and oneself. Among the primal hordes of bonobos and humans, concern for the other is always also expressed through caresses and sex; charitable love, by contrast, can permanently remain unilateral or at least asymmetrical. You love selflessly; the other may at best love you back for your selflessness. Even if you're the one who chooses the other, gives him shelter, takes possession of him, it is now he who absolutely needs you. Not wanting sex and tenderness protects the other from

8

unwanted intimacy, but it also protects you from ungovernable feelings and entanglements outside the one procreative union of man and woman—institutionalized in the form of marriage. The penis and testicles are utilized less and shrink across generations. Leftover sexual desire is masturbated away with the aid of fantasies and implements.

Humans domesticate not only animals (including themselves), but also plants and things. To hunter-gatherers, nature still appears animate, a power equal or even superior to their own; by contrast, in the forms of field, pasture, garden, equipment, and machine, it can't continue to exist without our ongoing care. Just as we distinguish, among our domestic animals, between farm animals and pets, we also distinguish between crops and decorative plants, as well as between tools and ornaments. Decorative plants and ornaments exist solely to be loved, but as we enjoy more free time and greater prosperity, our relation to crops and tools increasingly comes to be defined by love as well. They, too, become objects we shape and arrange so as to render them aesthetically seductive and avail ourselves of them only when we feel like it. Our taking possession of the world ultimately amounts to making it lovely. Functionalism is yet another aestheticism. Even nature that formerly elicited fear and disgust—beast of prey, plague, excrement, sex—seems to lend itself to imperceptible control. Only the technology that controls it threatens to become ungovernable and requires even more complex technology to keep it in check.

The question remains whether it is even desirable that humans should control everything. Tools can also be operated by other animals, or operate on their own. So our need to legitimate our rule propels us into an ever more all-encompassing love. Love and hatred usually help animals decide what to seek out and promote, what to avoid and combat. Human morality, by contrast, elevates itself above emotional instinct and determines what is even worthy of being loved or hated. The more we conceive ourselves as controlling our environment, the less justification we find to hate—after all, how things are is up to us. We might just as well be indifferent to our environment, like machines. But by cherishing, at least in principle, each bacterium and each grain of dust as highly as we cherish ourselves, we can maintain our superiority vis-à-vis both technology and all other life.

When the wealthy are serious about their charity, they strip their magnanimity of all personal and arbitrary choice, which provokes gratitude; they also renounce as many privileges as possible in favor of those in need or urge the introduction of equalizing taxes, education, and laws. The act originally motivated by charity becomes a bureaucratic regulation. Your love of your neighbor finds expression at most in the fact that you don't dodge this regulatory system, instead explicitly paying heed to it by speaking of, and meeting, the recipients of your subsidies with "politically correct" respect.

The more prosperity and free time we accumulate, the more pressing the question becomes of how charitable love may find expression. Perhaps there are countries where deep poverty remains prevalent and where you can provide immediate relief with personal donations—but the long-term effects are dubitable. We have only a limited understanding of nonhuman nature and it understands us even less, so any service we try to render to it always also patronizes it. We're fairly on the safe side only when we curtail human influence as much as possible by renouncing: by eating organic or, even better, vegan, consuming little, traveling rarely, and forgoing procreation. If you want something more combative, you can chain yourself to trees to protect them or throw yourself on baby seals. But most people live in cities and have few opportunities for such acts. To them, non-domesticated nature remains as abstract as the bacteria that their bodies coexist with.

In the meantime, there is a human need that tends to grow with rising material prosperity and the leisure that comes with it: the need for intimacy and physical love. Marriage feels less and less binding, and as everyone hunts for new and better lovers, the old, the ugly, the handicapped, and the unsuccessful get the short end of the stick. Sex can be bought, but sensual love is almost prohibitively expensive in an affluent society. Only someone who is famished can love another for a loaf of bread in return.

A right to love can't be institutionalized; the individual remains free to decide whether to honor it. Sensual charitable love is the opposite of regressive; unlike with free love, the point is to love, of all people, those whom you haven't felt attracted to. Charles Fourier and, later on, the hippies tried to revive the polyamorous primal horde as an elective community; the sensual completion of charitable love, by contrast, is about sexual love for those who are left over, whom no one wants. First, you've got to drill yourself to perform it. Instead of fighting emotions, habituation can engender them in the first place—the desired love—whereas hatred, like violence before it, is less and less excusable. You learn from hookers and gigolos to desire the other by making her or him desire you and so satisfying your self-love. If you can't pull it off on your own, you may also rely on the assistance of substances such as MDMA (more attraction), oxytocin (more attachment), and Viagra (more erection).

Since everyone finds their yearning for love promptly quenched, there is less and less room for jealousy as well as for hatred. Their place is taken by compersion: the happiness over the fact that the other finds more love than only yours. You don't love each other because you are desperate. You may be looking for the very special love precisely because you're basically provided for, and you're also able to find it without insisting on reciprocation. Insentient beings and objects—embedded in scaled virtual simulations, even bacteria—are especially suitable objects of fulfilled unilateral love, because they're impossible to rape or abuse. Sensual charitable love doesn't imply a new humanist essentialism. On the contrary, the extension of sexual love to people who don't meet our own standards is only the first step on the way to utterly unrestrained desire and sex also across the species barrier. Being alone with yourself or your species is now merely something you expressly want.

First Love

I could never sleep until I had labored through a regular lust application performed with motion, gesture, and languageflower. There was no script or dance step to the discipline. I administered it to her whether she was home in the head or away, no matter the score between her heart and the world, whether she swooned or cringed when I held her, or if she gazed into space or feigned sleep.

She received my application with short, gasping tones that she made with her own breath. The tones could have been stolen from a song. Every sound she made was borrowed from what was once known as music. It was not clear whether I should have responded with sounds of my own, which I had once used to pull people closer to my body, or any noise I could make to harmonize her noise into something passing for speech, which might then tell us what to do. Her sounds emerged most forcefully when the motion of my lust was piston-like, an event that often featured my person volleying above hers, as if flying in place, she pinned beneath me, wilting in my shadow; or me behind her, as though driving a chariot, while she carved a location for herself into the bedclothes.

When we pursued the discipline, we fought toward the seizure known as nighttime. Nighttime promised a better statistic of invisibility. It was our primary collaboration, to get somewhere where we wouldn't have to do anything else. We fantasized about a place where we could be wet and boneless, like water, where no one would dare attribute a feeling to us. The safest thing to say about water is that it has no bones, unless a person has been trapped in it.

She would announce her seizure some seconds before it occurred. She used American sounds known as phrases. She said "Here I come," and "Good Lord." I imagine the sounds she made once passed for words. When I announced my seizure, often by reciting her name, she held my hand. The sun was briefly refuted and I achieved a dark area. At such times I could see the two of us walking through a garden, looking at the world as though for the first time, believing that the flaring, bright obstacles that kept us from seeing deep into the earth were actually only called flowers.

In daylight she wore motion-limiting weights called shoes. She had a wet mistake buried in her chest. It should never have been put there. Someone had concealed a weapon, which helped her manifest a wound. She tried to sweat it free by performing a function called crying. The five knives of her hand were once called fingers. She stabbed her face every time she tried to eat; the cuts released small blasts of clear air that made the day feel cool. The flag of sadness that concealed her arms was known as a sleeve. The flag flew the colors of her body, which there is no longer another name for. The word "body" used to refer to the evidence left behind that someone had died.

The first time you meet potential partners presents an opportunity that will never come your way again, the chance to handle them freely, to smell their parts, to disrobe or possibly dismantle them, to mount their hind, to bark at them, to pull back their hair or grip at their scuff and whinny, to rope them to a post, to insert a wire into their back and control them through radio, to scull or tack in their perimeter, to kiss them gently, to hold their face and kiss their cheeks and shelter them with your wide, hard body from the wind.

Your appearance and behavioral strategy play a part in gaining this access to someone new, so it is imperative to keep your person clean and keep its tank and limbs filled with the appropriate water, seasonally correct and rich in emotion, to be sure its shoes are hard on top and solid for the long haul, to mind that your own person is posture-perfect and can aim its body true, accounting for the possible refractions of light that occur between the people of today, also known as the new wolves.

The shovels we use to cleave the air in two—and possibly reveal a person we might fail against—were once abbreviated as hands. This was when we had two shovels each, and we apparently used them to scoop up objects we thought we needed, or to toss away those that did not please us. When we faced off with a person, the sound of our four shovels colliding produced a shield of silent, wind-free air known as a home. This was when there were only two choices of how to behave: on or off. We would apparently put some objects into our mistake tunnel, which was still the main opening in the face, and the tunnel was able to convulse around them and propel them deep into the body's grave, which was then called, I think, a belly. The tunnel often became wet, but it had dry sticks in front known as teeth, to provide a final reflection of every object we buried in our bodies. Those people who wanted to consume us could then take an inventory of our assets simply by staring us in the mouth or, more obviously, putting their mouths over ours in an investigation known as kissing. Whenever she kissed me, she was prying for secrets.

My secret was my lucky bone, worn behind my face for good luck. It was an excellent protection against sorrow. Now seldom seen, at least in the daytime, this bone was once worn as an amulet above the neck to insure a human appearance; without it, a person might be considered a simple accident of light. It is a bone that grows in time with the body and achieves a round shape to best support the face. Some cultures call it a head and decorate it with paint and stones, or cover it with veils, gels, masks, and helmets.

In America the head sprouts either soft or coarse hair, features small apologies called eyes, and has a round mistake tunnel known as a mouth. The mouth asks for help by carving wind into short breaks in silence called languageflower. During escape tactics such as walking, the head precedes the person and falsely advertises its mood and what it might say. One of its functions is a decoy event called a smile. The head is better known as a flare for trouble. Some areas called cities feature millions of these flares hovering at eye level, and the effect is blinding. The Spanish word for this is "crowd." In America there is the phrase "Bury your head," which originates from the Dutch and translates roughly as "Hide behind another, enter the shadow, become married."

In some parts of America the little bone above a man's neck is considered to possess skills such as pain storage and escape strategies; the bone is suspended above the man as a charm against other people who would otherwise seize his body and pour themselves into it, a self-camouflaging sacrifice known as a relationship. But other people also use the little bone as a buoy that one should not approach, because someone will die in the space it covers. If you get too close to the buoy, you will be trapped as a mourner. Circling the head is referred to as courtship. It is like chalk around a body before that body has died. It hovers in place and appears attached to the fear spout that was once called a neck. In truth, every man's body is an announcement of a future disappearance. Just by being in the room with her, I was foreshadowing our separation. My head was simply the point where that disappearance would occur. If we ever need to know what will go away, we need only to look at a person.

Sometimes the disappearance can be traced. We conceal or disappear a part of the world and it's called swallowing. Many of the world's best objects, including the first engine—a fault called the heart— are hidden in the body. It is a competition to hide as much as we can, a form of self-ballooning that is believed, in some languages, to make us more attractive. We say we love someone, which means we covet or admire the hoard they might be storing in their bodies. While they sleep we try to reach at their hoard with our hands, an excavation better known as caressing. That is why lovers often say things to each other like "X marks the spot," "Come and get me," "I have a secret." Having a secret means: "I have swallowed part of you and that is why you feel incomplete." Massaging the skin is another way to feel for a secret entry. It is unfortunate that most people do not come equipped with a map and some cutting tools. So much time would be saved. Instead of saying "Pleased to meet you," we might make a small incision in the chest, wide enough for us to slip inside if the air will no longer tolerate our presence, if the population in the room is just asking for our omission.

In the current era, the male treasure hoarder uses someone else as storage space for his spoils, in case his own body is looted while he sleeps, a violation certain Americans still refer to as dreaming. There will then be a body or bodies that carry his assets after he has been found out. This grouping was once known as a family. People produced families to disperse the treasure and keep the sniper, who was once mistaken for a bird, guessing. In some American dialects, the word "family" means scatter. Having a family increases the number of targets, cuts the father's risk way down. With more people for the sniper to shoot at, the father has a better chance of getting out alive. His wife and children function as his bodyguards. This is also probably why relationships are referred to as bulletproof vests.

I had been advised by the Authority that a ritual at the outset of our union would at least make the relationship feel actual, which was then seen as a preferable condition. So I sent her some of the water I had blessed for the dedication of our relationship, telling her to have some of it to drink and to apply some as a lotion to the place she least wanted me to discover, so long as this place occurred on or near her own body. The water might protect her, even if I repeatedly touched her or looked at her, which was admittedly going to be my early plan. But if she spilled the water on her father, there would be a chance that I would kill him. It was a favor to warn her against my worst intentions. I wanted to show her my unsatisfiable side, to get the worst part out of the way, but it turned out that it wasn't just a side, but my entire body, and even the space around it that was unsatisfiable. Wherever I put my body, I left behind areas that could not be fixed. In a relationship every person gives a gift, usually by leaving something out. The best and most cherished gift is to give her the first clue as to why she should begin plotting her escape.

There are men blessed by water, whom women cannot see. This is the only favor water can grant, to cloak our mistakes by adding a layer of reflection to our skin, which helps other people take more responsibility for us once they see how horrible they can look when we reflect them. We have bodies of water, which are better known as failures of land, to show us where mistakes are made, because water gathers by nature near error, to magnify it and make everyone feel responsible. This quite natural atmospheric process was once understood as guilt. All the sorry men are laid out flat, ashamed to have ended up a mirror to other men. Dry men have made no mistakes. To look at water is to admit the possibility of error. Some men are still shy around water.

It was her belief that water, taken in drink form, would provide the necessary ballast for her to remain with me. But Americans believe it is unlucky to drink water, because those who do so will live.

The body will thrive and grow, and growth, particularly in English, implies movement away from others. The first word for it was "escape."

Commitment, on the other hand, is an abbreviation for an inability to move, which is why couples often become heavy together, stiff and slow moving, eating pounds of food to insure each other's immobility. Feeding a lover is like making her swallow an anchor. This is why getting married is described as swallowing iron. Marrying is never referred to as "casting off," although sometimes the phrase "taking on a passenger" is used.

Relationships fail when the mouth is too small or refuses food. Touching one's own mouth is the first gesture of masturbation, because it explicitly advertises self-sufficiency. Men grow moustaches and beards to become less attractive to themselves, to decrease the chances of making their partners obsolete. Cultures that eat with their hands are boasting about their love-making abilities.

I hoped to find the place she wanted to hide, and I suspected her place was hidden on another woman's body, someone who sulked in her shadow and answered to a different name. Thus an investigation occurred that featured me, in full color, sounding various skins for her secret place, an action more technically known as intercourse, because the man uses his entire body to listen against the skin of another. Often I was obliged to make lust applications to those host bodies that were possibly storing her mystery. Because I was intent on making the future come true, I looked for examples of her everywhere. The bodies that hosted my intercourse often overlapped with the bodies of the people she had once called her friends. They made altogether different sounds and words, and none of us could produce the sound that, in America, had come to pass for her name.

She sent back some of the water she had swallowed and it was clear that she had related to the water by letting it down her throat. This was water that had trafficked through her person to a place I had not been allowed to see. It had more access. I was jealous of everything she ate and drank. The water she sent back to me came in the form of rain. This was when changes in the air were known as weather, when low-flying bullets were still called friends, and periods of suffering were broken up into intervals called days. Back then, the sun still honored the world's objects by letting them contribute the occasional shadow to the surface of the world. Every day something fell on me and my temperature changed. Temperature was another way to remind you that you were only yourself and nothing else; it let you feel apart from everything around you. These changes of temperature were called moods and they had interesting foreign names, but I no longer recall them. I have no memory for anything that happens outside of my body.

I cannot recall the precise words for the phrase "I'm sorry."

When it was over, I was advised by the Authority to leap three times over a small running stream to prevent her forgetting me, after she had escaped from my house. Forgetfulness is a condition of the air, only slightly less common than the tree. It used to be called wind. A grounded person denies the air his body—he wears hard shoes, grows a belly, and carries lead weights called worries—and thus goes unknown, is carried nowhere, and is never brought to mind. Even the best and most expensive wind, from some of the most exclusive and rarest cities in America, can do little to this kind of ballasted man, who will never be lifted high enough for others to see him and thus come to know he is alive. At most, a woman will suspect that he is there, but the suspicion will never be confirmed.

ALEXANDER TARAKHOVSKY

The Indigestible Truth of Love

Inflammation

Clubbing. Not eating enough, or eating too much. Taking pills, smoking, drinking random liquors. Strong liquor burns epithelia cells in the esophagus. Damaged cells produce proteins that trigger inflammation. Inflammation is a beast. It can't stop easily and it makes a mess out of a thin layer of cells in the esophagus. Feeling under attack, inflamed cells attract migratory immune cells to defend and rebuild the tissue that, instead of being protected, is rattled and loses its natural color. The hopelessness of recovery strains cells and eventually drains their defenses against the damage. Mutations accumulate. Cells go Tahir, become disengaged from the rest of the tissue, and divide autonomously, eventually becoming cancerous. Cancer grows slowly but unstoppably, drinking becomes irrelevant, and at some point swallowing is an issue. Clubbing is not fun anymore, but perhaps it hadn't been fun for a long time. The walls of an apartment or a house unfold and the stage moves to the hospital ward. Colors fade progressively. Why do we need love?

Mongols

Out of a deep sleep he is extracted from a warm hut. Foxes and wolfs with glassy eyes are blotted against the dusty horizon. Two dogs and a pile of straw are in a front of the hut. Horses with bulging legs and earth-colored skin are graffitied upward, toward the sky above the hut.

When I was thirty-two, Lance Armstrong was diagnosed with testicular cancer. Too much bike riding did no good for the young man's genitals that got constantly squashed between muscular Lance's buttocks and a saddle. Lance and the rest of us are boreoeutherian land mammals with externalized testes. If Lance was a non-boreoeutherian mammal such as the monotreme, armadillo, sloth, and elephant, or even a boreoeutherian mammal with internal testes such as the rhinoceros, he would not have damaged his testicles, no cancer would ensue, and the Tour de France would snail into oblivion.

The boy's figure acquires the third dimension when he is lifted onto a horse. The father is behind him. Flatness expands in a light dimmed by dust. Father and son start galloping along the longitude dotted with decaying carcasses.

In mammals, the testes are contained within an extension of the abdomen called the scrotum. The average testicular volume is eighteen centimeters cubed per testis and normally ranges from twelve to thirty centimeters cubed. The average testicle size after puberty measures up to around five centimeters in length, two centimeters in breadth, and three centimeters in height. Human testicles are smaller than chimpanzee testicles but larger than gorilla testicles.

The horse gallops steadily with the boy wobbling around the spine. The boy's squinty eyes are pinned to the camouflaged landscape. He is a Mongol. Most noticeable are Mongolian folds around his eyelids, along with relatively high and pronounced cheekbones.

People with Down's syndrome were first called "Mongolian" in 1866. The World Health Organization officially dropped references to "Mongolism" in 1965 after a request by the Mongolian delegate.

The horse crosses the latitude of the future westward expansion several times and splashes dried puddles filled with excrement of steppe rats sick with bubonic plaque. After returning home, the mother will open the boy's legs and will grease the inflamed swollen testicles with the underskin fat of winter hamsters. Falling asleep, the boy feels nothing but pain and itching.

Inside the testicle, germ cells develop into spermatogonia, spermatocytes, spermatids, and spermatozoon through the process of spermatogenesis. Leydig cells, localized between seminiferous tubules, produce and secrete testosterone and other androgens important for sexual development and puberty, secondary sexual characteristics like facial hair, sexual behavior, and libido, supporting spermatogenesis and erectile function.

All of this is ruined by the constant rubbing against the horse's back. The winter hamsters' fat becomes a currency. Maligned by a testicular pain and shallow desires, the Mongols turn to the west and devastate it. They rape in despair, dicks hanging like pony tails, and fellow riders help each other mount their fermented bodies on women. They kill and lie on convulsing smooth-skinned female corpses, confusing gushing blood for vaginal fluid. They use stiffened phalluses of fallen horses sprinkled with anemic and pale Mongolian semen to enter wombs. The newborns are runts, with shifty watery eyes filled with the desire to kill or torture. All of this ordeal goes nearly unstoppably through Rostov, Uglich, Yaroslavl, Kostroma, Kashin, Ksnyatin, Gorodets, Galich, Pereslavl, Yuriev, Dmitrov, Volok, Tver, and Torzhok. In the west, Chernigov and Pereyaslav are sacked. Kiev, Poland, Hungary, Bulgaria, and Lithuania are fallen under lust-seeking Mongols. The horse penises are cut into thousands and rotten remains of horse corpses are catapulted inside sieged cities. Infections spread and most of the cities along the Tour de France route lose about two-thirds of their citizens to the outbreak of the bubonic plague. In their 1978 work *Atlas of World Population History*, Colin McEvedy and Richard Jones estimated that in 1300 the population of Russians in Europe dropped by five hundred thousand people —from seven and a half to seven million. Why love is so painful?

Ears

What time is it?

You've already been dead for thirty years; time must have little relevance for you.

It still does, but in a reverse order.

It's about four.

You sense time like a thief.

She was yelling at me and laughed hysterically because I ejaculated prematurely.

I could last for hours.

Was it "ears"?

Silence.

During my second time in the camp, a young Tatar doctor from a neighboring Mordovian city came to a prison and put five metal pellets in the skin around the head of my penis. We call the pellets "ears." The tissue around the "ears" would frequently get inflamed and the pellets would start to float like fish eyes inside bubbles of opaque puss. We would press the puss out by applying pliers, very gently, just enough to squeeze the skin around the pellet. To stop inflammation we would soak the penis in a cup filled with a tar-colored Georgian tea. The pliers would leave an imprint that we call a "wrinkly ear," like the ears of an old man burned by the sun, an old fisherman from Saransk.

After-your-death news. Gynecologist and surgeon Adam Ostrzenski of the Institute of Gynecology in St. Petersburg, Florida, reported in *The Journal of Sexual Medicine* the first anatomic evidence of the G-spot, which has been the subject of controversy for decades. "I am close to putting the controversy to rest completely," Ostrzenski told *NBC News*. Yet several respected sex researchers, *Science News* reported, including Beverly Whipple, one of the researchers who helped name the G-spot in 1982, are not so sure that he'd found it. "I have no idea what this thing is that he found," said Whipple, a sex researcher and professor emerita at Rutgers University. The skepticism is not unwarranted. It's not the fact that the study was conducted on an eighty-three-year-old woman and that the structure he found could be unique to her; nor is it the fact that Ostrzenski performed no other analysis to determine that the tissue he found really does what he claims. It's the fact that the new research was carried out on one woman: one—dead—woman. To find the G-spot, Ostrzenski dissected the vaginal wall of an

27

eighty-three-year-old woman who had died of a head injury less than twenty-four hours earlier. "The entire spot is very tiny," Ostrzenski said, according to *Science News.* Within a sac of connective tissue, he found bluish, grapelike clusters of tissue connected at the lower end to a ropelike structure. "Who is to say that this thing they found on her dissection was the center of pelvic pleasure?" asked Elena Ratner, assistant professor of obstetrics, gynecology, and reproductive medicine at Yale University, according to WebMD. Even more dismissive of Ostrzenski's claim is sex therapist Leonore Tiefer, clinical associate professor of psychiatry at New York University Medical Center. "We can conclude absolutely nothing from this paper since we know nothing about the sexual life of the dead woman," Tiefer told WebMD via e-mail.*

The prison guard was waiting for me in the tiny chamber filled with the vapor of the DDT insecticide. I felt nothing but she was catatonic after I had finished. I left her on a pile of uniforms infested with bedbugs and she gave me a key to her locker. I stayed inside until she came to change. She put me in a large training bag and carried me out of prison on a bus. While I was lying on the floor, she constantly touched my "ears" and I was afraid that they would get inflamed. She brought me home and I killed her after two weeks because my "ears" indeed got inflamed and she refused to buy me pliers from a German guy whose father has been sentenced to Mordovia by Stalin. Why is love selfish?

* Yukio Strachan, "Finding the G-Spot: A Doctor Puts Findings in a Study," April 25, 2012, *Digital Journal,* http://digitaljournal.com/article/323660.

Random Thoughts about Epigenetics, Physicist Anton Zeillinger, Dead Russian Poet Alexei Parshchikov, and Love as an Entanglement of Unconnected Events

Last night he was contemplating experiments that will prove the somatic memory of experience. A ball of hair was rolling through her stomach and she knew that it was her father's tumor. All of this blood spitting described by Dr. XX was narrated in the back room of a filthily decorated zaal just around the corner from the pension.

When I looked at the window, I saw a foggy street, oily cobblestones, and an angled silhouette of Lobachevski's wife. We went to Bashkiria last fall to drink the horse milk and to gather ancient gut microbiota. Edgar Allan Poe's wife was sick with tuberculosis that made her morbidly attractive with cerulean blue shadows under her eyes. The book title will be *The Erythroid Women and the End of Desire*.

Muslin, not to be confused with "Muslim," is a material; you squeeze your arm between the table and a heavy tusk-colored roll, push it with your shoulder while holding a meter in hand and, snap-snap, you fold the material to a size of the future dress. Many women in the nineteenth century liked to wear tusk-colored muslin dresses to emphasize their fatigued appearance and consumption-colored skin with an internal flair of inflamed blood. Dr. Blutstein-Oskerko offers the removal of bloodstains from bridal dresses using Chilean salts. Love is a disease.

Fatal Attraction

Tarik "Bloody" Morroy was sniffing cocaine in the back

of his van when he registered, with a corner of his eye, a rat that appeared at a far corner of the street next to the Starbucks. The image of the rat burned into Tarik's mind as cocaine sharpened his senses and put the time flow into the reverse of his heartbeat that was going about two hundred beats a minute. The rat was moving along the morbidly yellow pavement like a Navy SEAL in Kandahar with parts of it dissolving in the light only to reassemble against the grains of concrete. The rat's inconsistent appearance was driving Tarik mad because at this point he could not tolerate any deviation from a linear geometry. At the six o'clock position, a pit bull named after the slain nineteenth-century Chechen rebel Chamil entered the scene and was startled by the rat that displayed no interest in running away from its position at one o'clock. Tarik could see the air compressed in light-violet circles as Chamil cut through the space and annihilated the rat. At that point Tarik was already lying on the rubber floor with his heart going 260 beats a minute but he could see from the corner of his eye the rat's brain going down Chamil's esophagus, the nut-shaped cerebellum filled with Purkinje cells dissolving in small greasy puddles and the rest of the rat proceeding along the propulsion of pit-bull guts.

Tarik would be less surprised by the rat's behavior if he were aware of studies by Glenn McConkey of the University of Leeds, who found that *Toxoplasma gondii*, which infects 15 percent of the human race, can manipulate human or rat desires by making enzymes involved in the production of the molecule dopamine. Cocaine stimulates dopamine release, while haloperidol, an antipsychotic drug that Tarik got last year after some unpleasant episode that involved extraterrestrial voices, works by blocking dopamine receptors. Rats and mice infected with *T. gondii* get into a neurotic spin and fall in love with cats instead of running away from them.

And that's how the story goes. Ivan Turgenev jumped from a bridge into icy water somewhere in Paris to prove his love to Pauline Viardot. Turgenev had two cats in Paris and a bundle of feline runts waiting for him in a sealed barn at his estate in Russia. In the winter, cats get wild from hunger and breed with bacterial intensity to release their hunger lust. In the spring, Turgenev, who would return to Russia for hunting, opened a barn and fed morbidly anemic cats with freshly butchered wild-game meat and duck intestines. Dry cat excrement littered with *T. gondii* flew through the moist April air like freshly spooked dandelions to turn Turgenev into one of the most celebrated writers of his generation. Stalin loved Turgenev and most midget tyrants were used to massaging feline anal glands at night before giving somber morning orders to proceed with executions. Bugs drive love.

Theory

We love because we wish to survive.

We can't survive unless we mix our genes to gain temporal advantage against pathogens.

We can mix genes by casual sex, but in order to conquer cosmos or to be prepared for it, we must learn how to dream and that is why we need love.

We also need to mix our bugs and that is why we kiss and exchange fluids. Fluid exchange is disgusting but once you love, the evolution tricks you.

Art is like a bug for the brain. It inflames our mind like *T. gondii* and creates attraction to deadly creatures that nonetheless are useful facilitators of our evolution.

People who do not mix fluids, do not dream, and use hand sanitizer or mouthwash will be extinct.

Love is about mixing genes to compete with bacteria and viruses, and to dream together about conquering the cosmos in its various forms.

There's an avalanche of bloody news, yes, there's fear dispersed among people, there's these poisonous clouds over some cities, and nowhere to go, yes … we know all this and much more. We also know that there's order for the planets, and that tides are the generous breathing of the oceans … how does it all work, this balance, in spite of it all? How is it possible that we can talk to each other, two strangers suddenly communicating? Why are kids so fond of birds, and you and I of squirrels?

I think there's some kind of a glue that makes a table remain a table, the same glue maybe that makes it possible for us to read Nietzsche and get something out of that reading. Sometimes we feel like walking into the sunset, at other times we feel the need to hold a body against ours, and somehow it's all linked together, with that glue; I mean the tears and the bliss. Love exists; we can't define it, but we recognize it. It does exist. It's that special energy that keeps things together, and people together … it's all around, asking us to say yes to it. And why say yes to it, if not because it is there and because it is, in the deepest layer of our consciousness, the illuminated solution to everything that we live through. Love is the answer.

Getting Lucky

Sometimes people come up and from the beginning it's clear they're gonna break their own hearts. They're gonna ruin their lives. It's like suicide by cop. Keaton was on the roof of the church, climbed down, and told the cops, for no reason, "I have a gun." He said he was outraged he was in that situation. He knew he was better than the situation. They beat the shit out of him. Credibility is a basic survival tool. And building credit, for example, is a problem.

On his blog *Ribbonfarm*, the rogue consultant Venkatesh Rao writes, "You need good credit to get a loan, you need to get loans to develop good credit. […] In a general form, the chicken-egg problem is: *how do you get X, when you need Y to get X, and X to get Y?* There are at least four correct answers: 1. Slowly, 2. Painfully, 3. Unfairly, or 4. Untruthfully."

When you're trying to get lucky, these are the questions at hand: How do you get love when you need lovers to get love, and love to get lovers? And how do you love them, if you can't love all of them at once?

STRATEGY 1: SLOWLY
Fuzzy, Unclear, Biological Perseverance
We all know that there's no such thing as love without heartbreak. Even if you live forever and die at exactly the same moment, or achieve the big nightmare of living forever, together, somebody is going to be in pain.

Nevertheless, in the beginnings of love affairs, reluctance is the rule, the standard operating procedure.

Take it slow and you won't get hurt.

"I began to be involved with exercise. It was a little bit like sex sometimes—you know how sometimes you're kind of disinterested, kind of uninvolved, and slowly you begin to become interested? It's like learning to fall properly. If you can manage not to tighten up you won't hurt yourself as much," wrote Diane von Furstenberg in her 1977 *Book of Beauty.*

Taking it slow is the smartest plan. At the same time, we know this isn't really true. In feigning unavailability, you are manufacturing a scarcity. But you could undo it, if you wanted to. "We're both unavailable bitches," Maria said, "but we can make ourselves available."

STRATEGY 2: PAINFULLY
Use Money or Brute Force to Get the
Eggless Chicken or Chickenless Egg

This summer I got dumped for the first time. My contractual approach failed. The problem was that I didn't believe in the rules, but I also believed in them. One night it took me forever to walk out of the house. I was looking for my sunglasses out of habit. It was dark out, but I'd taken *Breakfast at Tiffany's* to heart.

"Obviously, you don't want to be this neurotic girl," Jessica Massa writes in *The Gaggle: How the Guys You Know Will Help You Find the Love You Want.* "And so, ever the proactive and logical modern woman, you want a solution. You want to 'fix' your love life."

Before I got dumped, I was the most sparkling young woman. I wanted Peter to fuck me, talk to me, and not be an asshole, in exchange for which I'd be

36

perfectly sparkling and comported. I saw our relationship unfold in front of me like a string of video-game coins. A procedure through which I would be rewarded. I knew I didn't exactly want the prize, but that's not what sportsmanship's about.

With my endless reserve of discipline, I was laboring under the belief that even though I knew the system was wrong, I should be able to win anyway—not despite, but because I knew better. I always had sense that by ignoring the rules, I'd be making an amateur error. And being too chicken to hear the advice is self-help's classic hook. Ingo refused to borrow my copy of *The 48 Laws of Power*. "What?" I asked, "are you afraid it's gonna work?"

The Girl's Guide to Hunting and Fishing is canonical chick lit from the year 2000. I read it seven times the year it came out. In the final story, the protagonist reluctantly internalizes a self-help book called *How to Meet and Marry Mr. Right*, which is "a terrible book"—terrible because it's so effective. Jane's recognition of the book's authors is total: I have known Bonnie and Faith my entire life, Jane thinks.

It makes her feel weird, but playing it cool works for Jane. She lures her love object onto an ultimately successful date at a play called *Mere Mortals* about bugs that live for twenty-four hours, mate, and die: "Leaving the theater, Robert and I are both dazzled and exuberant, talking at once and laughing, and we spontaneously kiss. He says, 'I want to mate with you and die.'"

When I called my mom to tell her I'd won an argument with Peter, she admonished me that it's not about winning, it's about successfully achieving your intention. You know, like in a studio visit. But when you're playing by the rules, what does success look like? Is it love, or the absence of pain?

ROSE	I just want the boyz to be falling all over me not sending coy texts
ME	word i feel u girl but they're all freaks its probably going to be a surprise ending, no matter if good or bad
ROSE	u rite u rite
ME	like w/e peter was just this chapter in my bildungsroman but something i realized after the fact is that i spent the whole time worrying about acting perfect to not mess it up. and like praying for it not to get messed up
ME	but like, i was doomed from the beginning so i shouldve had more fun with it
ME	lol not saying ur doomed but
ROSE	im not worried about being perfect about it just more like worried about feeling hurt

Ultimately, the moral of *The Girl's Guide to Hunting and Fishing* is that the painful route works, but only without great athleticism. Jane ends up being too lazy. "I'll lose him my way," she says. She goes from playing it cool to being cool, and they live happily ever after.

STRATEGY 3: UNFAIRLY
Sometimes Daddy Just Gives You a Job

There's a lot of freedom in being doomed. Knowing you can play perfectly and still lose frees you from having to play. Which is a big deal if you're worried about freedom.

> #115: *One way of loving people is to*
> *acknowledge that they have desires which*
> *exclude us; that it is possible to love*
> *and desire more than one person at the same*
> *time. Everyone knows this is true, and*
> *yet we don't want the people we love to start*
> *believing it about themselves. [...] I am so*
> *busy keeping an eye on the people I love that*
> *I have no time to be free. That is, I believe*
> *in my freedom but don't seem to want it.*
> *(Adam Phillips,* Monogamy*)*

Announcing your own death is a loophole, because it means you can live like this month is your last, go BASE jumping, and set off bombs in Egypt— and still chicken out at the end. A loophole is always unfair. It's asymmetrical. "I can't imagine this being okay for you," the one with more lovers, the noncommittal one, will say. "I feel like I can do anything because you love me," the suicidal one will say back.

The only thing to do if someone's broken heart is a certainty is to make it worth their while. But how? Make them teach you their certainty. Be exuberantly indecisive. And lie to them a lot; daddy only gives you a job if you're living like a loser to begin with.

39

STRATEGY 4: UNTRUTHFULLY
Fake the Chicken While the Egg Incubates

Once a boy was kissing me on the street saying "I'm in love with you I'm in love with you I'm in love with you" and it was freaking me out. I was like, "Stop saying that, stop saying that right now, cut it out." He looked bewildered. "C'mon," he said, "I didn't mean forever!" It was perfect. I was in love with him too.

"Say you'll be mine, say we'll be fine. Say we'll be together," Drake begs on the Justin Bieber song "Right Here." "Selfish of me to ask. Since I'll be the reason we don't last forever." It's the unbroken hearts that need reassurance, and to that end, the untruthful solution is a provisional "yes."

In the sixth volume of *Harry Potter*, Harry calms Ron's nerves before an important Quidditch match by slipping him a contraband infallibility potion called Felix Felicis. Molten gold in color, this "liquid luck" functions like the best self-help book ever. It whispers an infinite series of best possible scenarios in the minds of those who drink it—but leaves it up to you if you feel like listening. Only after Ron wins the game does Harry reveal that he hadn't in fact given him the real juice. Ron played that well all by himself. It was all Ron, all along.

When you tell everyone you love them, you commence an experiment in which the transformative power of your love is tested. Convince your lovers you have a gun, and wait to see if your lie gets manufactured into ammo.

Six Tales

Tale One

"Have you ever been a lover?"

"No."

He stares at me for a long time. I like it. He cannot decide yet if he is surprised or not by my answer. He is literally inside my eyes during the whole conversation. The question comes unannounced. A second ago we were talking about a performance.

"No."

My voice is lower than usual. I am thinking that his is such a great way of formulating the matter. The question is not if I ever had a lover, but rather if I have been one. He makes it into a privilege.

He was married to a woman for fourteen years. She contained him, his words. Not in the sense of exercising control: she was actually like a container. He was inside her and her ability of creating their common life. He was happy, till he, unexpectedly, fell in love.

"One reads in books about this complete different dimension of the sensual, of sexuality, of eroticism. I became an experience to myself. And I could not handle the wild surprise. There was nothing pleasurable about me feeling myself and her so intensely—to the contrary. I was suddenly living inside pure force. And violence took over. Every word I said was violent, every movement of my body, every answer, every question I posed, every decision I made, every word I wrote, eating, drinking, all was violent. Not even sex was different—violence was there too, together with something else, combined perhaps, but the most present element. I was inside transformation; I had no power over this power. I loved her violently, I wanted her and denied her. I made love to her and denied it also. I do not know how I came to tell you all this … I watched porn movies day and night, I masturbated neurotically. I tried to escape her somehow."

Silence.

"Yesterday, you mentioned the power of enigmas. Have you ever seen an apparition?"

"Never."

"I've been seeing ghosts. It was at this point of our relationship that I started seeing things. I heard voices. The voices came from the walls of my rented apartment, but I heard them in every place I moved through. As if my new existence was soaked in them.

"I did not know what to think of myself. A disorder, sure, due to the pain of hurting, to the pain of my inability with love. As my inability to deal with the immense pleasure of being with this other woman grew, the voices became louder and the presence of that something else more real. My horror was infinite and I had no idea how to conceal it.

"I replaced porn with horror. I began to watch horror movies."

His eyes are now all over the place. His voice is special. He speaks pure slowness, not slowly.

"In the middle of collapse and nervous eroticism, love was gaining a form, and it occurred while this frantic pursuit of the nature of fear—the fear of becoming mad—was also happening. Horror movies were like documentary material to me: in them I could

42

see my own experience. I understood all was related to me, it emanated from me. I was paralyzed and silent. I never said a word and they all thought it was divorce that changed me so drastically.

"I knew who they were. My own friends an I were beaten almost to death when I was nineteen. I survived though. They came back to perform these sessions of terror for me, while I was hoping for her to stay, to stay, to stay."

"And she?"

"She was all this terror. I love her."

Tale Two

He takes a seat next to me. He arrives before the time we agreed upon. He is nervous. I do not even know his name, but I know who he is. When we met yesterday, he said he missed the dinner the other night; he would have loved to have the opportunity to finally meet with me.

"Let's have breakfast then, tomorrow."

He turns red.

It was a weird moment. Some people were watching us.

"If you have time, we could meet at ten at the place where I am staying."

"How can I find you?"

The question is simply great.

"We just met. So, we will see each other again, but tomorrow, at ten, in another place, and, hopefully, we will recognize each other."

He looks at me. It is too much. He turns. He looks for a place to sit down.

I go to the desk prepared for me in the conference room. I spent the whole morning trying to think of what to say. Every time is worse. The tension was so big that I felt asleep. The call announcing the taxi waiting to take me to this place woke me up. I was late, my hair still wet. The notebook next to me is open on an empty double page. I hope to be able to take notes, as if I am to attend my own talk.

"I loved your talk yesterday."

"Thanks."

"Did you enjoy the dinner? I was at a great table."

I wasn't. "With whom?"

"My brother, and friends, you know all of them, and the woman you saw when we said good-bye at the end, my girlfriend, Laura. She says hello."

Silence.

"Well, you don't know her but she told me to give you her regards when I left the apartment."

"Your brother is an artist?"

"No. He is putting together the National Library. It's going to be great, he is great. I like my brother a lot. We were talking about you. Many people felt provoked by your talk."

"Many?"

"Sorry, I didn't mean it like that. At my table some were saying that it wasn't so new."

"I never said it was new."

"That's what I told them! I told them, I mean, that newness was not the point. I loved it. So did Josefina. It was special, yesterday. It was."

"But what did they dislike so much? What I said?"

44

"Well, they were saying it was not so new. But they were actually talking about something different. The way you performed. It was so intimidating. We all felt it. You did not stand up. You did not look at the paper once. You started talking as if you would never stop, as if the words were dictated, always staring at us."

"I was tired, my head a blank."

"You opened your speech saying you were completely unprepared. Your voice was all the air in the room. Finally you stopped. And then you mentioned that idea about the enigma. It was powerful."

"They disliked the idea?"

"No. They disliked you. Sorry, not you, but your manner. They thought you were intimidating."

"Why? I thought it was quite plain language, and the tone as well…"

"You never expressed a doubt, never a 'perhaps.' Your words landed in the room like real entities. We'd never experienced it before."

I am ill; my stomach is hurting. I am naked in front of those people, now in his words, yesterday. Somebody described this to me already. The somebody I love. These words sound like a situation scripted by him. Weird. I am in panic of crying before a stranger. I am in pain.

I cannot move. He looks at the window; he seems very nervous now. Me too. I feel miserable.

I look at him. He is handsome. Gray eyes, big. They have a strange boldness. He explained all this as if he could not stop his tongue, but he could. He is thinking of sex. He is thinking of oral sex. Why am I thinking this? This information enters my mind as a transmission. No emotions involved.

"Are you married?"

"Yes."

"Have you ever been a lover?"

Tale Three

I need a simple red lipstick. Red, a primary-red lipstick, then I can finally go to the hotel and dress for dinner. He has sent the address three times. In an e-mail this morning, a text message again at midday, and another e-mail in the afternoon, as a reminder. I had not responded to any of them.

There are at least ten to twelve make-up and lipstick displays in front of me, but I am unable to find what I want in the first nervous minutes. I am in a hurry; I decide to ask.

"I am looking for a red lipstick with no blue in it. You know what I mean, just the primary color."

She looks at me without understanding a word of what I am saying. I get impatient only by looking at her.

"It doesn't matter, I'll find it. Thanks."

She is running after me. She is talking. She is asking if she can be of more help. I do not turn around. Impolite.

At this moment, I am angry at myself. I cannot be nice, though, and she cannot help me. I spend some time studying all these hundred color bars. I am unaware of the time. I finally find it. I go to pay.

It is dark outside. I realize I spent two hours looking for a color. I am really late now. I have no other option but to reply to one of the two e-mails. I decide for the first, not the reminder. I am running late.

It is very cold outside, but bad temper helps you feel warm. I put a dress on, something really short, all black, no jewels. I fear the comments and am low on humor to perform any adequate answers.

Midtown. I have never been in the place before. The lighting is good. I relax a bit. They are at the bar. I leave my coat at the entrance and stay there for a few minutes. I can see them, but they do not notice me yet. He is talking about the south of Europe, I'm sure. He is comparing ways of life. He is praising, enacting the words with the hands, the face, the torso; for a second he is living a life more immediate, more vivid. He is an expectant man.

I walk toward them. She sees me first. She says my name, I say hers in reply. He steps back a little. I have no idea what to say. He gets a glass of red wine and gives it to me. She starts talking. Her voice is very nice. I only now look properly at her. They look alike. He is handsome, but she is not. The clothes are plain: jeans and a cotton T-shirt, flat shoes, a leather bag. All gray. Very expensive. I realize then, the place is expensive as well. I realize I look strict: my face is severe, my clothes sparse. The red lipstick adds a note. She is also thinking about her expensive grays. So, she attacks. Her brother told her about me, but she also knows what I do. She is a photographer herself, apparently a good portraitist. Her first question is about money. She wants to know how much I make a year. He objects. She smiles—she wants me nervous. But I relax. The attack suits me well.

"Enough not to need to marry rich. Joking!" I add. She is married to a wealthy man. She understands the counterattack and relaxes as well. She is smart. And he is, by now, completely lost.

The conversation lasts a bit longer but her mission has been accomplished and she leaves us. I say, "A pleasure," because I have no idea what to say. Alone now.

I say that I am not hungry. Neither is he. He proposes another place, an old-style place I fancy. He orders right away and starts talking at the same time. Food and feelings mix.

"You make me frantic."

I look at my plate now.

"You know, I cannot possibly sleep with you. I would feel weird. I never tried to kiss you for the same reason. I often think about sex, sex with you. I never met somebody I like this way. I am not talking about love, or not only. It is the material I am talking about. The first time I met you, you were leaning on a doorframe. I was not moving, staring at your back. You were talking to all the others seated on the sofa inside the room; it was a contest of nasty, funny remarks you were winning. I couldn't pass through the door, you didn't notice me, and I was hoping to be able to stay where I was for as long as I could. You then turned your head and saw me. We'd never met before. You did not seem to care and said my name followed by an order to join and sit with the others. I thought your face was something I was waiting to see all my life. I did not think it beautiful, I thought it right. And I was overpowered by the image, surmounted by the voice, and exceeded by the gestures. Exceeded, exceeded by the way your body was tilted and your eyes were staring at me. I was unable to read them. I had no idea if they were friendly or hostile.

"There is a force in you I know I can't win, if we were to have sex. I want to sleep with you. I want to have sex with you. But how this may happen, I still don't know."

Third glass of wine and the pain of not knowing an idiotic joke or comment is palpable. I am thinking about my voice. I am really worried now, not about the words, but about the tone. Whatever I say, it needs to sound able to convey an affect, a tamed intelligence.

I am not ready. I go for commonplace.

"I am married."

"Have you ever seen Lauren Bacall here? I did. I think she is still remarkable."

"I thought I did, once, but I am not sure."

"Perhaps, if you like what I do—I thought that if I show you things that matter to me, it may happen, I don't know. Would you come to Rio?"

"Sure."

Tale Four

He is late. On purpose. He knows I am there already and wants to gain as much control as he can over the situation. Tanned, dressed in an ice-blue shirt and dark-blue pants, he is pressing the car keys with his right hand in a very characteristic way. He knows he looks good—people are looking at him while he crosses the bar to join me at the counter. He has grown his hair longer. It is the color of wheat. He is so nervous that he needs to touch

49

it while walking toward me to release tension. I was in panic a minute ago. Now, seeing his hand strangling the keys, I am possessed by a humorous feeling of defiance.

"Aren't we very blue today?"

He wants to kill me but he is already laughing. Me too. I need to look at the floor in an attempt to stop myself. No success—we are both laughing almost hysterically. There is no joke in what I said. We have the same train of thought—I just render idiotic his choice of a shirt that's exactly the same shade as his eyes. The *pluralis majestatis* stresses this moment of vanity. It is all of a sudden very funny; we know each other too well.

"Pay. Let's go in the car. I think it's better than talking here."

We used to go for hours of driving and talking at night along the coast. He wants to rehearse it again.

"I shouldn't be talking to you."

"Don't."

"Shut up, you know what I'm talking about."

"Drive."

He starts the car and we go.

"I know my parents called you."

"I know it too. I talked to them."

"My father thought you would call me then, but you never did."

"I had nothing to say."

"I told them you don't give a shit."

He hits the wheel.

"I had nothing to say. It was your decision, a good one."

"Cynical. You are pure revenge."

"Revenge? Was I supposed to talk you out of it? I thought you really, really wanted to enter into that new identity, a new life. Everyone told me so."

"You could have tried to figure it out by yourself."

"I trust your criteria. Surely a good choice."

He is red by now. He is very angry.

"Listen, get out of the car."

"If you stop it I will, or I am supposed to jump out while it's moving?"

He stops it. I get out. I try to walk straight but I am very taken by the whole situation. He is just behind me, and I am scared of his reaction. He screams now.

"You know perfectly well that only your call could've stopped me! You deliberately chose not to!"

"What? I thought you wanted to become a policeman. Why not? The most promising art historian of the country joins the police force—I thought it was great! You were so fed up with the university, always despising them, their middle-classiness, their laziness, their lack of passion. I thought it only a logical consequence of your thinking, of your eternal confrontational attitude. Now you're saying you would've reversed your decision if only I'd have said so? Too proud to change your mind and appear to them as a clown, but you could've used my opposition to the idea as an alibi?"

Now I am screaming too. Louder and louder.

"But I thought it was great! Great that you joined the academy! Great that you even passed the tests! Anyhow you were an athlete—imagine how much they gained with you! You could swim after the drug dealers!! Esther Williams meets Sonny Crockett!!"

Silence. He is smiling.

"I am in the art-crime unit now."

His voice is particularly soft. He is standing right in front of me.

Again, we are both laughing.

"I am angry with you. You let me down."

"How?"

"You know how. Before I could react, you were married to that guy. I was speechless. We spent day after day together, never was a person closer to me, and you felt the same. You married to hurt me, to escape me, and you never gave me a chance. I went crazy. I even attended the wedding, in shock. And from that moment on, you just took revenge, moving away, leaving me alone, here, knowing I was not going to be able to go through it without you, without you containing me. Basically, I am only myself if I am with you. You took it personally that I never asked you out. Or so I think now. I thought you understood my reasons and saw, as well, that having a sexual relationship with you was impossible. It was clear, I was just sleeping with everyone, and at the same time, having a relationship only with you. I thought you understood. I would not risk starting a relationship with you only to then fail, losing you. I thought my only answer to your marriage was to abandon all we constructed together and become a policeman. I never thought you would allow me to do it. I was somehow convinced you would be scandalized, that you would romantically rescue me, that you then would invest in me differently, forcing me to become a writer to balance my uneasiness, to mediate between me and the world."

Silence.

I was looking at him looking at me.

He was very close to me, trembling, angry, and moved by some sort of love I was unable to relate to. I was very nervous too.

"You make me feel ugly."

"And I only can think of the future of art history being written by a policeman. I still do not know how to connect these two sentences, but I think you are in the right place."

He is crying now, quietly.

"Can I drive you somewhere?"

Tale Five

I arrived at the place he said, a bookshop with a café inside. He is there, already waiting for me. Very well dressed, his ugliness becomes an indispensable trait. Some say he works in television. I have no idea, I have never spoken long with him. He is the best friend of my mentor but we never talked about any personal matters. They are older than me.

"You did something to your hair."

His voice is memorable, unassuming, in place. He made this comment as if the change on my head was something one could overlook. I start laughing, laughing against my will. My efforts to prevent it did not allow me to answer.

"It looks great."

Again his voice showed no doubt, no irony, but his eyes were smiling. I was, by now, laughing loudly, without any idea why it was so funny. But it was very funny. He meant what he just said, and, at the same time, he did not. He sensed an alibi for the idiotic decision leading to a perm that looked beyond hysterical. He was somehow proud of the head that wears such a mark of the times, of the girl.

"It looks good on you. Perhaps you should reconsider the use of transparent gloss on your lips, though."

"Anything else I should reconsider?"

He is drinking what looks like water, but judging by the ice and the lemon must be a gin and tonic. Five cigarettes are on top of a notebook next to his left hand. He takes one, lights it, and starts smoking. He does not ask if it bothers me. It does not. It also gives me time to study his uncommon clothes. Gray tight jeans, a gray leather jacket that against all expectations looks credible, the strange brown pointy shoes, and a tight red sweater. He is very skinny, but he does work out.

"The shoes."

"The shoes?"

"Well, medium-height heels are no good. Use flats or high heels—everything in between makes no sense for you, I think."

"And?"

"No skirts with broad cardigans."

Silence.

"No bra to reduce the volume of your breasts. Color your hair darker, a tone or so. The chemical process burned it a little. Use something natural, no bleach."

He says all of this naturally, his voice and manner so gentle. The voice renders his words really true.

I stand up. He seems surprised, as if I woke him up unexpectedly.

"Where are you going?"

He says my name.

"I am sorry, I am stupid, please … where are you going now?"

"No worries, I just need to start following your advice. It's on my mind and I don't think I can continue to listen to whatever you want to tell me. Let's meet tomorrow, if you can. No literary coffee place, though."

"How can I find you? I'm not going to see any mutual friend that could pass you the message."

"I don't know. See you tomorrow."

He was still seated as I left him when I looked back from the street.

I am late and cannot find the room. It is a small one at the end of a particularly ugly corridor in this disagreeable seventies compound. I see five others through the glass wall. The teacher must be inside, since nobody seems to be talking among themselves. I enter. I hear his voice addressing me.

"Somebody left you a note."

I look in his direction. Three books are open on the table. Next to them, a flower and an envelope. All of a sudden I am terribly nervous.

"A young man left these two things on the table for you."

"I was unaware you were doing extra hours as a postman." My answer.

"I am not. I am helping two people in love."

"We are not in love."

"He said you would deny it. Since this is a

55

Hegel seminar, he stated it is all perfectly in context. So, please take the note and the rose, go to your seat, and let's discuss today Hegel's views on marriage."

What an idiot, taking all this effort to come to this place, finding out where I must be going. But I need to admit he is really getting my sense of humor.

The meeting is at midnight. The place: a very well-known club, a dance club. I see him leaning on his motorbike, the Montesa. Perhaps he intends to take it inside, to avoid potential trouble with this precious object. He is smoking and does not see me. Only when I stand right in front of him does he. I'd cut my hair and darkened it—my curls actually look good now. I have on a dress that looks like a man's shirt—silk, mint green. I look different. I look very different, actually. He makes no remarks. He stands up and makes a signal. I follow him. They seem to know him. We enter the place. It is so dark I cannot properly see a thing. It is clearly the start of the night. They are playing music, but the few people inside are mostly at the bar, not dancing. It is an old theater, a really alluring place. We go upstairs. We go all the way to the last floor. There is a sign saying RESERVED FOR THE STAFF. He continues upstairs. There is a central balcony and a room with a sofa, all from the late nineteenth century. He throws himself on the red sofa next to the balcony section of the space, as if exhausted. I take my coat off, and take a seat near him. He is lying, I am sitting. It is awkward. He covers his eyes with his arm. A person enters the space, says his name and leaves two drinks, two whiskeys it seems. "If you need anything, just press the button. The good music will start no sooner than one."

He is about to exit, but turns.

"Care for a line or two?"

"No! Of course not." He seems really sad that the man asked that.

"I better tell you what I have to say. Do not talk or make any smart remarks, it's not necessary."

I am so out of place already that I feel nothing could, actually, make me speak again, ever. I am completely mute, closed in my new dress under my stupid curls, behind my elegant nude make-up, intoxicated by my perfume, removed from my own decision of being here, with a person I barely know.

"I love you.

"I tried to forget about it. I left for a few months —I went to Germany. My friend probably told you I was gone.

"I love you. I love you and I know you are not in love with me. I even know you will probably never fall in love with me. You are not in love with anybody. But, I know I do interest you more than anybody. I see that I manage to intrigue you."

I move in my seat. I am not sure I am bold enough to move my arm, take my drink, and drink. I do. I start drinking it. And I notice the alcohol almost immediately.

"I am convinced we can become a great couple. You may think it not possible to have sex with a person you are not in love with. Even more so, given the fact that perhaps I may be the first one you will be having sex with … perhaps. That I don't know, of course. But, I actually think you are not of that kind. You may consider it even very convenient to have sex with somebody you do not love. I am not stupid, of course. I am aware of the role physical attraction plays and that certain conditions must be there for the fulfilling interaction between a man and a woman. I have been giving it deliberate thought."

I smile. I cannot help it. His last sentence is said in such a beautiful manner, as if it would be a matter of a historical unresolved equation. I know he looks at me once in a while when talking. It is like a tale—his voice tranquilizes me a great deal. I feel well.

"I think that even if you are not attracted to me, I can manage to make you feel really at ease with me through my use of humor combined with my love for you. True, it will never be passion on your part, but it may be better for a while, like a long warming up toward an understanding of sexual life."

I notice that I am really interested in his words, and really captivated by the way he says them. I do not want him to stop.

"You know, the other day I was thinking of giving you really nice underwear. I never thought about it before or even entered a shop. Not that I am shy, but actually because I never thought about the issue. But now I think it's important. The color, the softness. You are always hiding curves. I imagine these things you use—tight, opaque, uniform in texture, in color. Imagine it: if you would wear something a little bit less trustworthy as a material, something that would not hold your body in the way you are used to, you will then have no choice but to sense yourself. It is just a banal but effective exercise in self-eroticization.

"I thought of lying next to you, both of us dressed. And then with both my hands, slide your panties down, just a bit, allowing you to wonder if I will touch you with my hand. I see us lying there wondering what to do next. Me giving you time to expect something to happen, to think carefully about it, you—I am convinced—forgetting you are not in love, just getting excited, wanting me to go further."

Silence.

"Well, it's just an idea … that last thing."

Tale Six

He smiles. Next to him is another man, same age, mid-thirties, perhaps a little bit more. He looks at me and smiles as well, but one can tell he is uncomfortable. I kiss my friend and he introduces me to this guy, adding that he is his student. He gives me a hand. His hand is sweating. It makes me nervous. Together they look like oil and water, and yet, there is a strange commonality among them.

He refers to him several times. I thought it's weird he accepted private lessons. I thought of a gifted child. Now, I don't know what to think. He is too old to be a professional musician and I do not see the point in wasting time teaching a person playing for pleasure. Strange. The student is wearing a suit. It looks expensive: dark blue, well cut, with a white shirt. However, something is not quite synchronized in him. The shoes, perhaps. They are too chunky, bulkier, like the ones schoolboys wear in French movies rehearsing some historical nostalgia. The size of the suit. I do not know where exactly to locate the discomfort. His clothes look as if they made a decision not to dress him.

From now on, the student will appear on every occasion. They all act as if he is not there. But he is there—I notice his presence. He does not say much and is always gentle. He seems to enjoy our company but this seems so unlikely to me. They all spend hours talking about music as if it were the auto industry. They go on and on about the sound of instruments, the presence or the lack of echo. He smiles at them all the time. It is as if he provides them with a perfect pretext to engage for hours in such boring talks. I do not know what to do. I am mostly there because I want to see where all this is going.

My friend calls. He says we are all invited to his house. Dinner. He adds that it is going to be a formal dinner. The student requested that all dress up. I do not understand. I ask if his friends are also attending the party then. He says, "He has no friends." I am not surprised by the statement, but I am not pleased either.

"Are you going to dress formally?"

"Of course."

He finds it great. I listen to his instructions and say, "I will be there." I have no intention of going, though.

The doorbell is ringing. Weird. It's quite late and I'm not expecting anybody. I feel observed all of a sudden. It rings again. Uneasiness is all over my body now. I hear my name. I know the voice—it is the student. He repeats my name. I answer, surprised: "Yes?"

"I came to pick you up. We all thought something must be the matter and I thought it best to come by."

Silence.

"They are all at home, waiting for us. It is going to be great. Do you need much?"

"Give me five minutes, please. I'll come downstairs."

My head is empty. I go to the shower. I do not know what to do. Before I can think of something, my hair is wet. Stupid. I have no time to blow-dry it. I put on a black velvet dress. It was given to me. My boyfriend gave it to me. I never had it on before. A tight black velvet dress. Not my taste. It fits perfectly. I think of a violin player. This outfit is the worst. The dress is open in the back. I need to hide my bra. My hair is wet. The curls look impossible to sort out. I tie it into a ponytail. It doesn't work. I cover my head with a black scarf, à la Gloria Swanson, and apply a coat of make-up to my skin. All together, it looks terrible.

I go downstairs. He is wearing a tuxedo. He is finishing a cigarette next to a car with the lights on. His car. An expensive car in a dull color. I go in. He is nervous. He says I look incredible. I believe him. I don't say a word. The others are enjoying a bottle of champagne and his new sound system. He just got it from the States. "It is very expensive," he adds, "but it's worth it." We are heading toward the north part of the city, where wealthy people live.

What is the occasion of the invitation?

He seems surprised.

"You don't know?"

"No."

"The loudspeakers!"

"The loudspeakers."

"The loudspeakers, yes. I ordered them right after one of the first meetings with your friends. They all were mentioning this new sound system and the possibility of rehearsing at home and it sounding like a concert hall. They are extraordinary objects, you know. Almost like music instruments. You order them and they are handmade for you. It took months, but they finally arrived on Monday."

"Monday."

"Yes, but I needed to call somebody in London to come over. Someone from the company in London to properly install them. It is crucial to do it right, otherwise the effort would be useless. I bought tons of new music as well. They are all ecstatic."

We are now in front of a modern apartment building, no more than three stories high. A fence around it, a garden, probably even a swimming pool.

The fence opens. He parks in a garage under the building.

I get out.

He gives me a signal to go toward the main door.

"I need a minute—I'm carsick. Which floor is yours?"

"The third, the top floor. My name is here." He shows me the buzzer. His name is there, the student's.

He stares at me, dismay in his eyes.

"I'll come up in a minute—just need air."

He goes. I see how he enters the elevator.

I see a small door, my exit. I am in the street now. I start walking opposite the building. If they look through the windows, they will not be able to see me. I stop a taxi.

I take off my scarf. I say the address of a friend. I cannot go home—too scared he will come after me.

The next day I go home at noon. I pack my things and go to the airport. I've needed to do this trip for a long time. Now it seems perfect. It is Sunday and there is nobody at the airport. I have two options, London or Brussels. I try for Brussels, and it works.

I am carrying a bottle of wine and a bunch of books that makes it difficult to open the door. My friend opens. She can see me through the glass door. She is smiling. She is wearing a short skirt and high heels.

"Are we going out?"

She laughs out loud.

"Nee, nein. No," she translates. "I cooked dinner and I thought just to dress properly to my food."

I take the books to my room. The table is ready. The wine served.

"Somebody called for you today."

"A name?"

"No. But he came by later and left a package for you."

I do not quite understand what she says and yet, my whole attitude is defensive.

"It's quite big. I'll bring it to you."

It is a very big box. I open it. I open it with fear, as if a corpse or a part of a corpse is inside. Two other boxes are inside. They have numbers. 1 and 2.

I follow the numbers without thinking. My friend is drinking wine and watching the scene in silence. Number 1 contains a music player. Shiny, pale blue—it is a beautiful object. It is a very expensive object. "A present," she says. A present.

My face must be white, because she does not add anything to the remark. Number 2 is a CD case. Billy Joel.

I'd never heard of him, but my friend had. There is a Post-it note in the booklet inside the CD case. My friend has already one of the CDs in her hands.

I go to the page the Post-it indicates. I see the lyrics of a song. She sees the song title as well, and inserts the CD into the music player. It plays.

Whole sentences are marked. Some words are encircled.

> *She can wound with her eyes. She only reveals*
> *what she wants you to see. She can lead you*
> *to love. She'll carelessly cut you. She can't be*
> *convicted. She's always a woman to me.*

There are three circles around this last sentence: one blue, one green, the outer red. The sound of these words is now loud. I cannot move.

"It is a love declaration."

"I do not want his love."

"But you know him, right? You must have seen this coming."

"I barely know him. He is a student."

"A student?"

"A music student of a close friend, yes."

"A music student."

"Well, no. He is a banker but he took private lessons."

"Of Baroque music?"

"Of Early Music, yes."

"Early Music. Well, it's the same to me.

Billy Joel is not of that era, though."

"No, not of that era." I just repeat her words.

"He could have sent you something else if he is interested in your music, in you."

Yes, he could.

"You saw him?"

"I saw a man in a suit. Nice brown hair, brown eyes, good looking. He spoke perfect English, but he had a soft Spanish accent. However he spoke with a perfect British intonation. He said he got the address from a friend of yours. He was in town for a few hours, work matters. He had wished to see you. I asked him to wait. He said he had to take a plane."

"A plane. I hope he is back."

"I guess so. Dinner?"

I'm dialing the number of my friend. I'm screaming at him. Did he give my address to a stranger? He fails to understand my anger. I am out of control. I fail to understand his attitude.

I open the door to my apartment building and I watch my back while I turn the key.

I have been away for almost two months. There is a pile of envelopes on top of my mailbox. I take it all with me.

It has been a few days since I've been home and I am calmer. I call my friend. I apologize for my reaction. I have not seen anyone yet.

I feel like throwing away all the mail. But I don't.

The last thing I open is a very large envelope. It contains floor plans. I look at the address again: I must have taken the mail of my neighbor. It was sent to me.

I unfold the thin papers. They are floor plans of what seems to be a house. There are numbers in several of the spaces and a folder with papers. Inside the folder there is a cover letter, handwritten, and a second page. The second page has a list of numbers on it and a question attached to each number.

> 1. Kitchen floor:
> *Would you prefer tiles? Wood?*
> 2. Kitchen cabinets:
> *I thought Bulthaup. A plain color,*
> *preferably light.*
> 3. Living room + bedrooms, floors:
> *Wood? Thought of whitened beech.*
> 4. Restrooms:
> *Drummonds.*

I go to the letter. It starts: "My love."

He knows he is going too fast, too soon. He knows I am not in love with him. He believes I am not in love with anybody and thinks it is the best of all possible worlds for love to survive when one is in love and the other is not. This condition of seeking and avoiding is described in his letter and is desirable, ideal. He says the pain is worth it, since it brings with it the solution many are dreaming of, the solution to a long-lasting relationship. Lack of love with love is indeed much better than corresponding love. Since I, the woman, happen to be the one not loving, I may make the mistake of thinking this perspective he presents is impossible. If the woman, I, would be the one loving, she would articulate the whole situation around the notion of "hope."

A hope supported by the thought that it is always possible for a man to sleep with and, eventually, fall for
a woman who is, without doubt, attractive. However,
the reverse case may seem now, at the present time,
aberrant to her, to me, to the one holding this paper.
My disgust, he argues, is caused by my impossibility
of imagining sex with him. It does not need to be. He
would insist on us marrying. We should share a life, a
house, a bedroom, but not intimacy, or not immediately.
It is not necessary to him. My presence is, but not sex.
He is no saint, but he can get sex where he always has
gotten it, in brothels. He would prefer to break this
habit, but he's come to think it's difficult to sleep with
people he does not want to share his life with, unless he
pays. He's found a person, me, and he is ready to give,
to respond with commitment, to engage. He is ready
for love and the sacrifices it entails. Nobody said the
solution would be an easy one, but he's found it.

Douce

Somewhere in a D. H. Lawrence essay there's an aside about the easy vehemence with which lovers hate and revile each other after their relationships are over. It's something that has always struck me as odd and inhuman. If you loved me then, why do you hate me now? If you were close to me then, why are you far from me now? Why does the time element—that simple transition from one moment to another—change everything? If our love was so right then, how could it be so wrong now? If our closeness was correct then, how could it be misguided now? How can intelligent humans allow mere perspective, mere position, to determine the substance of their judgments?

The reference is from Lawrence's 1930 essay "A Propos of 'Lady Chatterley's Lover.'" I'm going to weave bits of it into the text. I like his rhythms, his emphasis, his repetitions.

> *The peculiar hatred of people who have not loved one another, but who have pretended to, even perhaps have imagined they really did love, is one of the phenomena of our time. The phenomenon, of course, belongs to all times. But today it is almost universal. People who thought they loved one another dearly, dearly, and went on for years, ideal: lo! suddenly the most profound and vivid hatred appears. If it doesn't come out fairly young, it saves itself till the happy couple are nearing*

fifty, the time of the great sexual change—and then—cataclysm!*

For Lawrence, this facile callousness was evidence that hearts were wired wrongly in the modern world—an immediately intriguing answer for me. I'm drawn to people willing to condemn modern etiquette, people able to reveal the ideology hidden in habit. The cynical, hostile explanation for the thunderous silence of my approximately three hundred ex-lovers (if they were beside me then, why can't they be beside me now, all approximately three hundred of them?) would be that I am somehow sick, and that the approximately three-hundred-fold silence is in fact one single, simple, unspoken sentence: We are silent, we are absent, because you are a douche.

"Douche" isn't a word I use. In fact, the word—callously, dismissively simplistic—represents exactly the kind of savagery that Lawrence was talking about.

> *Nothing is more startling. Nothing is more staggering, in our age, than the intensity of the hatred people, men and women, feel for one another when they have once "loved" one another. It breaks out in the most extraordinary ways. And when you know people intimately, it is almost universal. It is the charwoman as much as the mistress, and the duchess as much as the policeman's wife.*

We call someone a douche when we want to place rhetorical distance between our behavior and theirs, ignoring, denying, and suppressing the fact of our common humanity, projecting actions we dare not own up to in ourselves onto the other. "Get over him," people on a message board tell a spurned lover, "he was always a douche." It's meant kindly, a device by which the addressee can salvage an ego badly damaged in an emotional car crash. But implicitly it also says, you made serious mistakes of judgment, taste, and understanding when you embarked on that relationship, mistakes that you can only now erase by suspending all empathy for the person involved. It's much too obvious and easy a strategy. If she was wrong then, why should she be right now?

Encouraging a bruised friend to reject and character-assassinate an ex is cold comfort, because if the former understanding of the situation was incorrect, why shouldn't the current understanding prove, in time, equally incorrect? Does it really help a friend when you encourage them (so transparently, so patronizingly) to think in ways that salvage their good opinion of themselves, rather than think in a clear-headed and realistic way? Wouldn't a real friend give you their real view, one based on substance rather than position?

For Lawrence, brutality and sentimentality were two sides of the same coin:

> *And it [hating] would be too horrible, if one did not remember that in all of them, men and women alike, it is the organic reaction against counterfeit love. All love today is counterfeit. It is a stereotyped thing. All the young know*

just how they ought to feel and how they
ought to behave, in love. And they feel and
behave like that. And it is counterfeit love.
So the revenge will come back at them, tenfold.
The sex, the very sexual organism in man
and woman alike accumulates a deadly and
desperate rage, after a certain amount of
counterfeit love has been palmed off on it, even
if itself has given nothing but counterfeit
love. The element of counterfeit love at last
maddens, or else kills, sex, the deepest sex in
the individual. But perhaps it would be safe
to say that it always *enrages the inner*
sex, even if at last it kills it. There is always
the period of rage. And the strange thing is,
the worst offenders in the counterfeit love game,
fall into the greatest rage. Those whose love
has been a bit sincere are always gentler, even
though they have been most swindled.

Well, I'm probably expecting far too much
from mere human beings. Of *course*, after a difficult parting, we try to salvage our ego by all means
necessary. Of *course*, after an unhappy ending or a
deeply hurtful rejection, we can't think objectively.
And of *course*, if we're to create anything new, we must
demolish the twisted, tangled wreckage of the old.

I can't help loving the prophets—the D. H.
Lawrences, the R. D. Laings, the Martin Bubers,
the Erich Fromms—who don't say "*He* was wrong,"
but "*We* are wrong." The preachers who tell us we are
sick, collectively. That we ought to be stretched out on

the psychoanalyst's couch, as a whole society. That we went wrong in Britain, or in the nineteenth century, or in our nuclear families, or in our child rearing, and that now, as a result, we are schizoid, unable to love correctly. I admire people who shepherd us away from the savagery of the *douche* view and toward the softness of the *douce* view. I think it takes a very great bravery to be tender-minded.

Now the real tragedy is here: that we are none of us all of a piece, none of us all counterfeit, or all true love. And in many a marriage, in among the counterfeit there flickers a little flame of the true thing, on both sides. The tragedy is, that in an age peculiarly conscious of counterfeit, peculiarly suspicious of substitute and swindle in emotion, particularly sexual emotion, the rage and mistrust against the counterfeit element is likely to overwhelm and extinguish the small, true flame of real loving communion, which might have made two lives happy. Herein lies the danger of harping only on the counterfeit and the swindle of emotion, as most "advanced" writers do. Though they do it, of *course*, to counterbalance the hugely greater swindle of the sentimental "sweet" writers.

In the *douce* view of my past relationships, the sentimental view, I still love everybody I have ever loved, and not one iota less than I ever loved them. If they are not here with me now, physically, it's because they've each been so firmly introjected into my psyche that they seem to be with me all the time. It's not necessary to be with someone you've partly become. The way I sit on the bus with my knees squeezed up against the seat in front? It's something I learned from A. The way I answer praise with a comically arrogant "*Of course!*"

73

rather than standard demurral? It's a tic I learned from B, and when I use it reflexively, B might as well be in the room with me.

Facebook is another way I can maintain the illusion that the approximately three hundred have not deserted me, because some of them have friended me, or at least not de-friended me. From the glowing blue-and-white page I can glean tiny filaments of connection even to those I'm not friended to, thanks to Facebook's baroque and ever-shifting privacy settings. Ah, C has "liked" a singer called Herb Diamante! So I go off and listen to this track he recorded with the Sun City Girls, and feel the artificial presence of a person I haven't seen for five years. Facebook—with its weird use of the noun "friend" as a verb, and the verb "like" as a noun—gives me a comforting illusion that I can continue to draw warmth from functionally defunct relationships, though of course it falls far short of my wish for real continuous connection with every one of the approximately three hundred.

But do I really wish for continuous connection with them? I couldn't have had approximately three hundred lovers if I'd loved each one of them enough to forestall the action of leaving, of moving on. My desire to maintain connection is pure sentimentality. And, as Lawrence knew, that sentimentality is not incompatible with the callousness of my approximately 299 abjurations.

I know the rules. The rules are that you can only have one partner, one sincere and serious emotional investment, at a time. Which means, practically, secretly, two partners at a time: an official and visible one representing official monogamy and an unofficial, invisible one representing the desire for polygamy generated, precisely, by this official monogamy. By rebelling secretly against monogamy we confirm it. Our cock and our bull collude.

The truth is that I play my part in maintaining those approximately 299 silences, and I do it conscientiously and considerately, to give each ex the space she needs to make a new investment, to concentrate on a new love. It's creative destruction, a pact of hygiene. It's the price we pay for the collective decision to love, officially and visibly, only one person at a time.

The hurtful silence of exes is the price we pay for official monogamy. I endure approximately 299 absences because I appear to value above all else one presence. Yes, it's somewhat unrealistic. Yes, it's rhetoric, and yes, it's revisionism. It airbrushes people out of history. It voids the cache.

Ask your partner, "If we were to split up, would you stay in touch with me?" Don't assume that the only acceptable answer is "I hope so!" Perhaps "No!" would be the most loving answer. Perhaps a heart can be exited for the same reason it was entered, and through the same wound. Perhaps a heart can be abjured for the same reason it was first embraced.

To my approximately 299 exes, I would therefore say this: I am far from you now for exactly the same reason that I was close to you then. That reason is love. The one love. The total love. The love that therefore excludes much more than it includes. Totalitarian love. Political love.

And to the question posed before about time changing everything, I think the answer has to be this: The time element changes nothing about love. If I recognized something worth loving in you then, I still recognize it now, and I will recognize it in the future. All that changes is my commitment, my official position, my public statement. Because, in a totalitarian world, every lover has to be a bit of a politician.

Everybody on Earth Is Feeling the Exact Same Thing as You: Notes on Relationships in the Twenty-First Century

It's very hard to imagine phoning someone up and saying, "Hey, come over to my house and we'll sit next to each other on chairs and go online together!" Going online is such an intrinsically solitary act and yet, ironically, it allows for groups to be formed.

* * *

I think it's very funny the way even the most nice-seeming people turn into trolls and monsters when they go online alone at night. Anonymity unmasks them.

* * *

Last year at a conference about cities I met this guy from Google who asked me what I knew about Fort McMurray, Alberta. I told him it's an oil-extraction town in the middle of nowhere, and because of this, it has the most disproportionately male demographic of any city in North America. Its population is maybe fifty thousand. I asked him why he was asking and he said,

"Because it has the highest per capita video-streaming rate of anywhere in North America."

* * *

Dutch researchers doing a survey of the effects of pornography on men had to cancel the study because they simply couldn't find a man anywhere on Earth who hadn't, at some point, sought out porn. They were trying to find an "uncontaminated" statistical control pool and had to abandon their project.

* * *

I don't know if women go online looking for porn. It's hard to imagine them doing that. They must think men are pigs. But they must do *something*, even if it's just a fantasy of making it with the tradesman who installed the new stove.

* * *

I think that because of the Internet, straight people are now having the same amount of sex as gay guys are always supposed to be having. There's a weird hollowed-out look I can see on the face of people who are getting too much sex delivered to them via hooking up on the Internet—or anywhere else, for that matter. They've gotten laid but there's a whiff of failure to it all. *Is this it?* I find that younger people of all types are highly aware that too much sex will desensitize them to love. In the old days they never had that option. So that's totally new.

* * *

Back on the old *Mary Tyler Moore Show*, Lou Grant asked Mary how many times a girl could be with a different man before she became "that kind of girl," and Mary thought about it very carefully and said, "Six." Some psychologists have come to the conclusion that most people have five or six "loves" and once they use them up, that's it. Sixes get used up very quickly in the new information world.

* * *

People in the pornography industry have found that the magic price point for people subscribing to a porn site is $29.95. The moment you cross that line, potential customers balk and leave. This is called "the porn wall" and it seems to be an impenetrable thing, and a constant that's built into us by nature, like the nesting instinct of birds or the molecular weight of zinc.

* * *

In the 1990s there was a thirty-year-old Latino guy who passed himself off as a hot teenage girl in a Florida high school and spent a year and a half there before they found out. I think he attended his PTA meetings as his own father. I think that in certain ways, we've all become Latino guys pretending to be hot cheerleaders—except maybe you're not pretending to be a cheerleader, you're pretending to be a studly cowboy or whoever it is you wish you could be to the person on the other end who has no way of disproving it.

* * *

Sometimes people really connect online, but, of course, they live far away from each other. So, ultimately, one of them buys a plane ticket and flies across the country to meet the other in person. If there's no physical chemistry it leads to one very depressing drink and some desultory conversation before they both go home. People in the dating industry call these people "next-flight-homers." Sometimes people really connect online and when they meet in person they physically click. People in the dating industry call them "room-getters."

* * *

I sometimes wonder about people who wake up and spend almost the whole day online. When they go to bed at night, they'll have almost no organic memories of their own. If they do this for a long time, you can begin to say that their intelligence is, in a true sense, artificial. Which I guess means sex lives have never been as artificial as they are now.

* * *

People seem to be pickier about bodies these days. New high-definition TV cameras have changed the way we look at bodies. Even a faint acne scar looks like the Grand Canyon on a high-def screen. TV casting agents have started to heavily favor actors with perfectly smooth skin. It's like the dermatological equivalent of the introduction of sound into film in 1929.

* * *

It's more pressure than ever for movie stars to look and be a certain way, and it's hard growing old in the modern world. It's hard to imagine Jack Nicholson with Alzheimer's. David Bowie is going to be seventy soon. I don't know how I feel about all of this. At least online you can fake youth—you can fake everything.

* * *

It's only when you don't have an Internet connection or lose your phone that you realize how alone you are in the world. I don't know if I'd want to go back to being 1992 me or 1982 me—all that time I spent being largely isolated and alienated.

* * *

I don't think people being on their devices all the time is an indicator of social isolation. Maybe it's the opposite. In Manhattan about one person in three on any given sidewalk is using a device. Some people say that's bad because they're not "in the moment," but I think it's kind of nice because you have visible proof that people need and want to be with other people.

* * *

I watched *Looking for Mr. Goodbar* a few weeks ago. It was Richard Gere and Diane Keaton in 1970s New York and I was horrified by how low-tech it was back then. It's like people lived in badly furnished caves connected by landlines. It was a real eye-opener.

* * *

Once you get used to a certain level of connection, there's just no way to go back to where you were before. The thing about 2013 is that people are more connected than they've ever been—except they've been tricked into thinking they're more isolated than ever. How did that happen?

* * *

I find that whenever I stay with people, the first ninety minutes of the day are spent online collectively waking up the way we used to wake up with newspapers. Every morning when I open my e-mails, there's a part of me that feels like I'm scratching a lottery ticket, except instead of just winning things, you can also lose things, too. Money. Friends. Status. Work. Love. It's the best moment in the day for many people—that delicious three-second window when, after reading all your papers and blogs, you say, "Ahhhh ... and now I'm going to check my personal e-mail." Because it's all about *you*.

EVA ILLOUZ

How Bondage Solves the Problem of Modern Love

Have you ever had sadomasochistic fantasies? If you're like me, not only have you never had any, but you even view sadomasochism as an exotic and very distant land. Assuming that most people are boringly similar to me, then it's a puzzle how *Fifty Shades of Grey*—a 2011 romance novel by E. L. James in which BDSM (short for bondage and discipline, dominance and submission, sadism and masochism) is the central plot motif— became a phenomenal global success.

Many commentators have too easily solved the puzzle by calling it a result of and testimony to a main-streaming of porn culture. What was previously hidden in the stash of magazines under the bed, and more recently in private Internet browsers, has become legitimate. But soft-porn literature has been around for a long time too, and the range of sexually unconventional behaviors is wide; so that justification does not explain why this particular novel, with a BDSM relationship at its center, has garnered such uncanny success. The *Fifty Shades* trilogy has sold more than seventy million copies worldwide, and its rights have been bought in thirty-seven countries and counting. It is flying off the shelves faster than the Harry Potter books.

Unsurprisingly, the book has elicited fierce feminist controversies in the United Kingdom and the United States regarding the question of whether submissiveness is a violent or emancipating fantasy for women. But, as a cultural sociologist, I suggest that before we engage in a discussion about the politics of the book, we should try to understand why it provides pleasure—of the symbolic rather than sexual variety.

Best sellers are always a puzzle. Most of the time, no one predicts their success; yet, once they do succeed, it's as if their success was inevitable. How can we now explain that the new worldwide best seller *Fifty Shades of Grey* not only succeeded, but did so despite its mind-boggling flaws as a piece of literature?

To a sociologist, a best seller is defined by its capacity to resonate with our social experience in at least three different ways: it contains very familiar aspects of our social experiences; it addresses—in a veiled or explicit way—an aspect of that ordinary experience that is difficult, elusive, and a source of constant bafflement; and it offers a symbolic, fantasized resolution to this bafflement.

Fifty Shades has the structure of a very conventional romance. The story is set in Seattle and focuses on Anastasia Steele, a college girl who is still a virgin when she meets the very attractive, successful, and young Christian Grey. For the first time in her life, she experiences intense sexual desire and finds in him an exceptional sexual partner. Indeed, something sets him apart from other men: he will enter a full relationship with her only if she signs a contract in which she willingly agrees to become his "submissive"—that is, she agrees to be beaten, spanked, and tied up, to lower her eyes in his presence, to sleep the number of hours he prescribes for her, and to eat the foods and wear the clothes only he chooses for her. In addition to this contract, she is also asked to sign a nondisclosure agreement preventing her from divulging to anyone the nature of their relationship.

With these elements, the book represents a perfect mixture of a very conventional romance with an intensely charged erotic novel centered on a BDSM contract. This is familiar territory. Since the eighteenth century, romance novels have given expression to women's search for love using the pleasurable formula in which the heroine meets an attractive but dark and threatening man who later reveals himself to love and be devoted to her.

Fifty Shades also treads on another familiar terrain as it raises the now-obsessive question of the role that free sexuality should play in women's lives. It is a question largely popularized through such TV series as *Sex and the City* and, more recently, *Girls*. Sexuality in its many forms has also become a familiar theme through the process, which some have identified as the "pornification" of culture or the mainstreaming of pornography in culture.

In *Fifty Shades*, the familiar search for love and good sex is used to address the endlessly baffling question that has chiefly preoccupied psychologists, sociologists, artists, writers, and ordinary people: What do men and women want when they are together?

The relationship that progressively unravels between Christian and Anastasia displays their gendered and divided desires: "I don't do the girlfriend thing," he says repeatedly, in addition to "I don't make

85

love … I fuck hard." She, on the other hand, is preoccupied with her intense desire for him, struggling to
make sense of his aloofness and mood swings as well
as her endless self-doubting and surprise at being
desired. "His sudden aloofness makes me paralyzed,"
she thinks. "He wants me?" she asks.

But each wants the same thing: for the other
to desire him/her exactly as he/she wants. "I need him
to want me like I want," Anastasia tells herself inces-
santly, whereas he ceaselessly says, "I want you to want
to please me." Each wants to remain free, and each
wants to enslave the will and the desire of the other.

This is indeed the Hegelian conundrum that
modern sexual and romantic relationships labor around,
often hopelessly so. This is also why romantic relations
have become full of ambivalence (replete with conflict-
ing emotions and desires), of uncertainty (we never
really know what their rules are, or what their outcome
will be), and of indeterminacy (poised between the
casual and the committed, the painful and the pleasurable, the secure and the anxious).

In *Fifty Shades*, these endless conundrums are
solved by a sadomasochist contract that at first seems
deceivingly like an obstacle to love. Moreover, I would
argue that the sadomasochist relationship in general
is a highly plausible solution to the complicated and
uncertain labors of love for a number of reasons:

– By definition, a BDSM relationship contains both
  pain and pleasure and thus neutralizes the ambivalence of relationships that alternate between pain
  and pleasure.

– One of the greatest difficulties of modern relationships is relinquishing one's autonomy to another because, in doing that, our sense of dignity is always at stake. The BDSM contract does the logically and psychologically impossible: it makes one willingly give up one's will and autonomy to another. In that sense, it solves the problem of relinquishing one's autonomy.

– The equality that has been promoted by forty years of feminism demands ongoing, ceaseless negotiation. The BDSM contract stops the endless bargaining by setting up and freezing caricatured and exaggerated roles and positions. In fact, BDSM makes inequality acceptable because it is consensual, contractual, and pleasurable.

– Finally, sadomasochism can take place only between two people who fully trust each other. The dominant partner stops hurting the submissive partner as soon as he or she says the code word. In that sense, BDSM is the very performance of the scarcest commodity: trust.

Against this context, it is our ordinary heterosexual relationships that have become queer indeed: complicated and elusive and impossible to predict and control. They demand an enormous sophistication in our capacity to play many roles, endlessly negotiate boundaries, and make sense of our own and the other's ambivalence. If conventional relationships have become queer, then the romance between Grey and Steele suggests that

BDSM actually holds the promise of erasing that queerness by giving us access to erotic ecstasy without the anxiety of ambivalence and uncertainty.

BDSM: a utopian, normal relationship for our times?

BEATRIZ PRECIADO

The Contra-Sexual Manifesto

CONTRA-SEXUAL CONTRACT (SAMPLE)

I, the signatory _____, hereby forswear, by my own will, body, and affects, my biopolitical position as a man or a woman, any privilege (whether social, economic, or regarding hereditary rights), and any commitment (whether social, economic, or reproductive) resulting from my gender, sex, and race within the framework of the naturalized heterosexual system.

I recognize my body and all living bodies as speaking bodies and I fully consent to never enter into a naturalized sexual relationship with them, and to never have sex with them outside of temporal and consensual contra-sexual contracts.

I declare myself a somatic translator: a dildo-producer, translator and distributor of dildos onto my own body and onto any body signing this contract.

I renounce all the privileges and all obligations that could derive from the unequal power positions generated by the consensual use and re-inscription of dildos within the framework of this contract.

I declare myself as a hole and as a worker of the asshole.

I resign all legal kinship (both parental and marital) that has been assigned to me within the heterosexual regime, as well as all privileges and obligations derived from them.

I resign all property rights over my sexual fluids and cells and over the production of my uterus. I recognize the right to use my reproductive cells only within the framework of a consensual contra-sexual contract. I resign all property rights over the body or bodies produced within the context of a contra-sexual reproductive practice.

This agreement is valid during a period of time of _____ days, _____ months, and _____ years.

Signature

Date

CONTRA-SEXUAL INVERSION PRACTICES

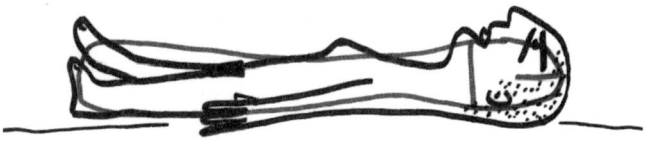

gode-total

Dildotectonics

Dildotectonics is the experimental contra-science dedicated to the study of the birth, formation, and uses of the dildo. Here the term "dildo" designates all kinds of technologies of gender and sex that resist the normative production of the body and its pleasures. Dildotectonics's aim is to draw a general cartography of the cracks and slippages inflicted by the dildo on the hegemonic sex-gender system. To make dildotectonics a critical branch of contra-sexuality is to consider the body as a *dildoscape*: a living surface where dildos are inscribed and displaced.

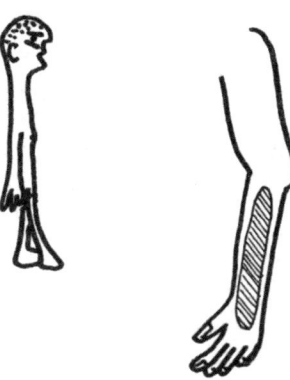

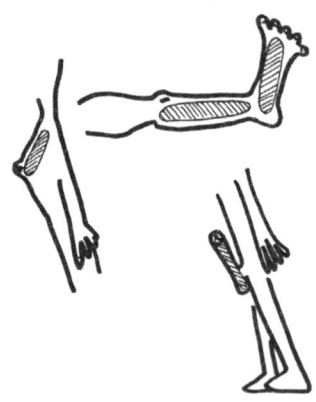

Within the heteronormative regime, the term "dildotectonics" describes deviant and non-normal uses of the individual body, or a practice where several bodies make gender or have sex with dildos. Practiced by subaltern subjects, and working against the medical and psychological discourses that naturalize the body, sex, and sexuality (and according to which the dildo is a "fetish"), dildotectonics is not an easy science.

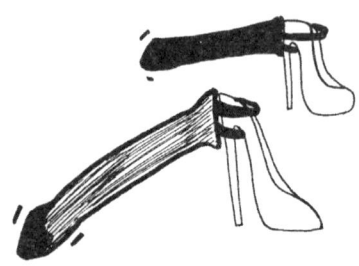

Dildotectonics locates gender and sexual technologies of resistance. It studies their functioning, the ways in which they interrupt the flow of production of body-pleasure capital not only within heterosexual but also within queer cultures.

The notion of "dildo" can be generalized to reinterpret the history of philosophy and art production. Thus, within Jacques Derrida's grammatology, "writing" is the dildo of the metaphysics of presence. Likewise, following Walter Benjamin, within the era of mechanical reproduction, a museum is always a collection of dildos. Finally, all philosophy can be traced back to a more-or-less complex dildology.

Dildotopia

Within the heterosexual and capitalist regime, the body functions as a total prosthesis working at the service of sexual reproduction and the production of genital pleasure. The body is organized around a single somato-semantic signifier that must be mechanically excited over and over again. This definition of sexual activity, both heterosexual and homosexual, is deathly and death driven.

The aim of this contra-sexual practice is to modify the ordinary uses of the sexual body, subverting their biopolitical reactions. This exercise is based on the practice of grafting new meanings onto certain body parts using the operation of dildotectonic *inversion* and *investment*.

The double term *inversion/investment* refers to an operation of textual-prosthetic citation that overturns the hegemonic syntagma of the heterosexual regime. First, drawing from an economic term, *investment* refers to the action of supplying a surplus of energy or biopolitical meaning onto an organ expecting the production of a counter-benefit. It is a practice of sharing bodily energy and biopolitical meaning within time. Thus, the individual body is no longer private property but *shared*. Second, to *invest* implies to endow a certain body part with new performative force, conferring authority to do something else, or to produce otherwise. Third, the invested organ is physically covered, redesigned. *Inversion* means not only physical reversal, but also the reaction causing a change from one biopolitical configuration of the body into another, opening the possibility of new uses of the self. This operation of citation displaces the performative force of the heterosexual code to invert/invest the body, causing a perversion, a dislocation of the effects of sexual activity.

Practice No. 1
Masturbating an arm: citation of the graph "dildo" on a forearm

Principle Directing the Practice
The dildo logic

Technology
Contra-sexual translation of the dildo on a forearm, or dildotectonics applied to an arm

Number of Bodies (or Speaking Subjects) Who Take Part in the Practice
One

Materials
A red marker

Optional Material
A violin (or an approximate imitation of this instrument)

Total Duration of the Practice
2 minutes, 30 seconds

Description of the Practice
A speaking body holds a (real or fake) violin between its jaw and its left shoulder. The left hand touches the strings with precision. The right hand agitates the bow with energy. The eyes look to the left arm as if the score were written on the skin.

Without changing the position of the body, the violin is removed from the arms (operation: cutting out the violin). The head, now without the violin, rests on the left shoulder. The place occupied by the violin is now taken by a dildo. The action is not an aim in itself, but is a transitive movement.

The operation of somatic translation takes the dildo out of the left arm (operation: cutting out the dildo). Then a dildo shall be drawn onto the forearm's skin with a red marker. This practice comes from the techniques used during phalloplasty surgery (surgical construction of a penis) using the muscles and the skin of the forearms or the legs. Contemporary medicine works as if the body was a plastic and open landscape where every organ can become some other organ, something else. Taking into account this somatic plasticity, every body potentially contains at least four penises (two on the legs, two on the arms) and an indeterminate number of vaginas (as many holes and folds as can be artificially opened within the body). This body is no longer transgender, but contra-gender.

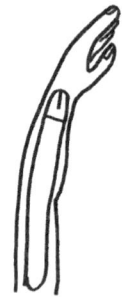

The eyes move now toward the forearm's skin where the dildo has been grafted. The right hand grasps the dildo-arm and slides up and down, intensifying blood circulation toward the fingers (operation: jerking off a dildo-arm). The left hand opens and closes rhythmically. Blood circulation becomes more and more intense. The effect is music-like. The melody is the sound produced by rubbing the skin. The body breathes following the rhythm of friction.

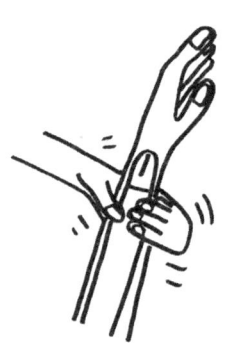

The total time must be controlled using a chronometer that indicates, arbitrarily, the moment of pleasure and the orgasmic climax. Orgasm must be simulated during ten seconds. After that, breathing becomes calmer and deeper and the arms and the head are totally relaxed.

Practice No. 2
Citation of the graph "dildo" on a head

Principle Directing the Practice
The dildo logic

Technology
Contra-sexual translation of the dildo on a head, or dildotectonics applied to a head

Number of Bodies (or Speaking Subjects) Who Take Part in the Practice
Three

Materials
A red marker, 75 ml (nontoxic) red-colored water, an electric shaver

Total Duration of the Practice
2 minutes, 5 seconds

Description of the Practice
Three bodies (or speaking subjects) sign a contra-sexual contract with the aim to get to know and to improve the practice of citation of the graph "dildo"

on the head. The practice will be performed as many times as considered necessary in order for all the bodies to be placed, at least once, at the citation position.

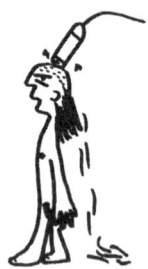

First, two of the bodies shave the other's head. The operation of somatic translation is performed through the citation of the "dildo" on the surface of the shaved head, drawing a dildo sign on the skin with a red marker. The body situated at the citation position takes seventy-five milliliters of red-colored water into its mouth. It stands up between the other two bodies. The working bodies will rub the dildo-head, rhythmically sliding their hands up and down. Every forty seconds, the dildo-head will spit red water, looking at the sky. After two minutes, it will have ejected water three times. Immediately after the third ejaculation, the body placed at the citation position will utter a piercing cry simulating a vehement orgasm.

The contractual practice of shaving heads (operation: removing hair, undressing the head's scalp as skin) can be performed over several days, during which the three bodies learn and practice the technique of citation of the graph "dildo" on each other's heads until they become experts in the art of provoking and simulating head orgasms.

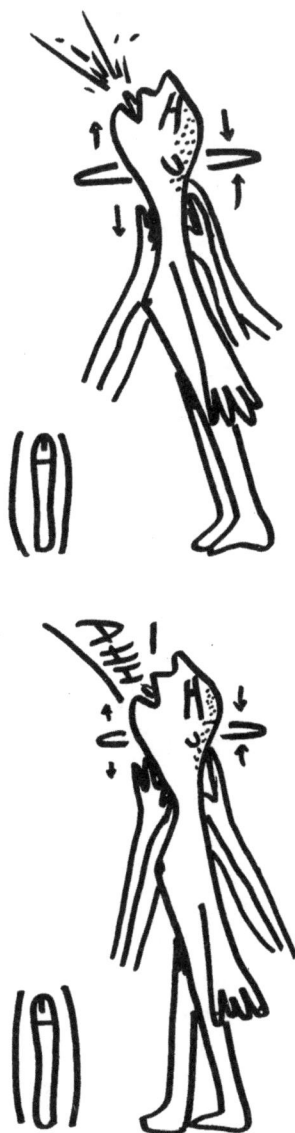

The Completists

Summer daybreak. Rare birds twitter on the Rehwiese in the Zehlendorf district of Berlin. The one-and-a-half-kilometer-long grassy strip is one of the glacial meltwater channels formed in the Ice Age. The grass in most Berlin parks is already scorched, though here it stands tall in a luscious green. In a strong rainfall the Rehwiese quickly turns swampy, since the Berlin waterworks only pumps out three million cubic meters of "sweetwater" annually and not nine million like it did in the eighties.

The Rehwiese, or "deer meadow," onto which deer still dared to venture at the beginning of the twentieth century, was severed from the Grunewald forest by a highway. It can hardly be heard in the meadow valleys, but in front of the high row of villas that line its entire length, a roar, as gentle as it is constant, blends in with the rustling of the trees.

All of the villas were built in the late nineteenth century; occasionally though, a little postwar building has been squeezed in between. All of the houses are in good condition and occupied. The paintwork follows the historical original and ranges in color from antique white to sandy yellow. The buildings achieve a homogeneity through the sallow hues that allow one to overlook the often sizeable tangle of bays, balconies, rooftop elements, and even towers and framework.

Often the villa architecture is even more playful in Grunewald and by Halensee lake. The use of natural stone and timber framing is more common, the towers more commanding; some houses resemble the castles at Disneyland. The Rehwiese bourgeois is less inclined to knightly structural shapes than to those of the squire. He is more modest and frugal. Doesn't loot, but earns. Doesn't have people killed, has them work.

A last Rehwiese villa was freshly restored after years of vacancy. A family of four now resides in the ground floor, first floor, and attic. The front half of the basement was converted into an office with room for up to ten employees. They can eat in the approximately twenty-square-meter common room in the back. It only has one small window on the side, soundproof. A ventilation pipe is next to the window. This way, despite the low ceilings, even larger crowds of people smoking can hold out for longer periods of time and make as much noise as they want.

What remains of a larger evening party has retreated into this room. Almost all of them are approaching forty or have already past it. Two tables stand in the middle of the room, though all are lounging on and around the pillow-covered ledge surrounding the entire space. Despite the ventilation, the air is dull with smoke. A few candles provide the light and are used as cigarette lighters. The music ended a few minutes ago. No one feels like pulling themselves up to start it again. Sometimes you can hear the buzz of the refrigerator and ice machine.

"Where is Bruno?"

"Upstairs in the little tower, smoking."

"And Nicole?"

"Helping Ulf carry something."

"Is that the ambition?"

"What?"

"Summer shower, summer cuisine, vegetable patch, and herb garden."

"And the blooming magnolias in the spring."

"Late summer picking of blackberries on the Rehwiese."

"Biannual trash collection. What comes together there: curtain rods, exhaust pipes, a Swiss passport."

"Honorary battle against the Japanese knotweed. The *Berliner Abendschau* news reports."

"Middle-class Arcadia."

"Securing the VW Golf with a steering-wheel lock. Getting a haircut at Hair Globe, but feeling as if you would live next door to the Great Gatsby."

"Are you jealous?"

"Or are you thinking: That's *our* money?"

"Bullshit. They really earned it. And even if they didn't it wouldn't be so bad."

"You don't pass judgment. Wise, wise."

"That's how he sneaks in others' heads and never resists himself."

"But what do you do with all that stuff, with other people's thought-junk on top of it all?"

"Sell: and to whom, may I ask? It's much better to wait with the idea snatching until the other one has already attempted it, to see if it works out."

"That's why there's no new house?"

"Where in Germany would you build that anyway? But here: the highway ramp, the subway station. In a maximum of a half hour you're at any spot in the city. Maybe not at eight in the morning.

But luckily the law offices and art galleries aren't open yet then."

"But you've got the noise."

"You won't get a building permit in the middle of nature anyway. Maybe they'll let you build on the foundation wall of a burned-out barn if you pull a few tricks. Then you get really strange floor plans, like at Botho Strauß's. And even he lives within earshot of the highway. Also in the shadow of a cellular network antenna."

"I like the highway noise. My parents live close to it, too. As a child I thought it was great that I could get to the highway bridge so quickly. Where else do you feel such a large, wide, clean width?"

"It's embarrassing that Ulf has joined an initiative for better noise control on the Nikolassee. Someone should buy up the remainder of his sports-car books from Merve and dump them in the lake."

"But Ulf lives a lot closer to it."

"And a few in the initiative live so close that when the wind blows the wrong way, the cigarette butts tossed from passing car windows land on their lawn."

"But that's also a much more radical drive, when you're surrounded by a five-meter-high noise barrier. I think we should tunnel all of the highways completely. And all traffic in the city should be underground."

"Isn't cheap."

"But it feels so good. Haven't you ever driven through the new tunnel under the city? When I suddenly came out on Potsdamer Platz, I really had a flash for one, two seconds."

"What were you *on*?"

Peter stands up and puts "Ring of Fire" by Johnny Cash on repeat.

"America is just bigger. Still."

"And if you hit a border, then it's the ocean. Even further. Even more to explore."

"Pioneers don't live in America anymore either."

Cecily stands up and changes the music. 50 Cent, "P.I.M.P."

"Hippies, Hell's Angels, Merry Pranksters, even yuppies, nerds, and all of this hip-hop shit. That still smells like freedom. And in Europe? Mods—uptight. The communist groups and the RAF were the same. The only thing invented here was totalitarianism."

"The Vietcong as the new Indians. And the Taliban: American-trained cowboys."

"So you see it can't go on like this. That's the reason for the new bourgeoisie: a reimport from America. Frank Schirrmacher tries to conquer the Donner Pass as a creation myth for the new middle-class family."

"One of the few great examples of occidental cannibalism. The only survivors were the ones who didn't refuse human flesh. They were mostly the families and especially women and children."

"The single men were easier to sacrifice than the family men. You would have had to kill the wife and the kids as well."

"Maybe only the men knew what kind of meat it was, which is the reason they refused it. Just like the two Indian guides that were also shot and eaten."

"The women knew; they cooked the meat so that their children would have a future. That was a good pretense for keeping themselves alive by any means necessary. The same was true for the fathers."

Sarah stands up now to change the music: Ennio Morricone, "Addio a Cheyenne."

She returns to her seat, stretches herself out and says, "There was a time when we took the greatest expanses into our possession. We were carried by legs that were not our own. We killed the things that stood in our way and took what didn't belong to us. We took everything over and divided it into lots. We hit no borders but a garden fence. It is time to return. But others have long occupied the place that we came from. We have to leave and relinquish without substitution."

"Why *us*? What do we have in common with the pioneers?"

"No movement is possible without that silent 'we.' Whether or not those included are dead, sluggish, blind, or discouraged doesn't matter."

"Wouldn't it be more honest to contain this unity in the 'I'? The 'I' can ultimately embody even more than the 'we.' Everything."

"And how much can you chop off and still be you: both eyes, hands, arms, legs, ears. A kidney. Breasts, penis, testicles. A piece of liver. Skin and blood too. Hair."

"All the wheelchair-accessible bathrooms or jobs for the handicapped are thanks to rigorous legislature derived from fundamental rights. Formulations like 'differently abled' are a natural diffusion of the law into language. But socialism was a workers' movement and not a cripples' movement. The communes that had free love wouldn't have taken in old people, morons, and spazzes. The humanists are preaching the intellectual perfection of mankind. But what about the ones that are too stupid? What remains to be seen is a revolution that really includes all people."

"But then there would be no more opponents to it."

"No opponents on principle. There are only the not-yet-converts."

"This revolution is actually a sect."

"A revolution that isn't grounded on the fight against somebody before doing something good. One that won't eventually have to resort to desperate measures because the objective can't be met and becomes irrelevant. Reform and revolution have to become one—because reform is already so drastic and revolutionary. The 'battle in heaven.' We have to set up a boutique where we offer old, ugly, and handicapped people free sex. We ourselves."

"We call it charitable prostitution," Cecily says, who has stood up to put 50 Cent's "P.I.M.P." on again.

"First you have to learn to appreciate prostitution. Not just as a personal pleasure or lesser evil. There are people who would never be able to have sex were it not for prostitution. Who, even more so in earlier times, wouldn't have been able steer into the safe harbor of marriage. Who would never be able to manage having sex on their own, not even masturbation. In their desperation they clutch a wardress's shoe and lick it a little bit. Then there's a scolding."

"Prostitution is only okay if both sides possess a healthy self-confidence. Meaning they're convinced that they could also get money or sex, respectively, some other way. They both just find prostitution particularly comfortable or pleasant."

"That's why it's so important to offer it free to handicapped people."

"But isn't that even more humiliating for them than to pay for it like normal people?"

"We have to offer them more than just sex."

"You can't force love."

"Every child *must* be loved by its parents."

"That's where the hormonal programming comes in. But with adults and complete strangers it's something else."

"That's why we have to get to know them. Then we *have* to just be helpful to them, in every respect. We have completed altruism. Two thousand years after Christ. That will change our society completely. The winos, the homeless—everyone will be made happy."

"And if they fall unhappily in love with us? Try to rape one of us?"

"We always perform as a group. Linger about them, finger ourselves, get warm and let them get warm too. They shouldn't feel overwhelmed by us either. They have to want it."

"Good."

"Okay then."

The group walks up the cellar steps and into a radiant morning. Nicole and Bruno water the fresh plantings.

Bruno asks, "Are you having breakfast with us?"

"Another time."

"That was a great party. Thanks a lot."

"See you soon."

"Just give me a call and drop by."

The group gives Bruno and Nicole hand-shakes and cheek-kisses and makes its way ahead to the Rehwiese.

Dana says, "We always have to keep moving. At twenty-six I had already traveled to fifty countries. Then I stopped counting. Even the inward journey is at most only another destination. Not uninteresting, but definitely not as complex and surprising as an entire country."

Cecily says, "I bought myself a piece of waste-land in Mecklenburg for less than a thousand euros. I bought the Internet domains for my name with every possible ending. My shoplifting career ended with a warning."

Chris says, "My parents died young. I devel-oped a guilt complex more comprehensive than that of Holocaust survivors. I was still so little then. Every breath is guilt."

"Would you like to be raped by a handi-capped person?"

"That wouldn't be rape then."

"If you were killed?"

"Then I would be too much of a coward to do it myself."

"And why don't you?"

"Because that would only distract me from my guilt."

"So are you trying to do the opposite by living as long as possible?"

"The only thing that I can do is to die in such a way that I stay utilizable. They shouldn't just be able to keep using the organs, but like with the Nazis, the hair, fat, and everything else too."

"What are we doing now?"

"Looking for handicapped people."

"Where? I have no idea."

"I was in Pankow recently. There was a newly built workshop for the handicapped right on the Bürgerpark. Also a dementia clinic—maybe it's not too late for a few of their patients. We can get there from the Nikolassee station."

"Okay."

The group continues on to Spanische Allee, then a few hundred meters further to S-Bahnhof Nikolassee. On an information panel they read, "A real estate company financed this station's construction in 1902." Sweet-water Station. They get on the S1 to Oranienburg, ride past Grunewald, Steglitz, and Schöneberg, plunge under Potsdamer Platz and emerge again at Humboldthain in Wedding. After a good forty minutes they step off at the Wollankstraße station, walk along where the wall once was until they reach the Delphin workshop for the handicapped. A salmon-colored functional building with green window frames, pitched roof, and a glass-covered porch. The lawn in front of the building is used by employees as a parking lot.

They see the association's name and symbol on the sign on the door: SOCIAL SERVICES OF CATHOLIC WOMEN.

"Crap, this'll be hard."

"Those exact people are our enemy. The ones who have absolutely de-eroticized helping. The effects of that can be felt all the way through psychoanalysis."

"And they're women, which means they don't even have underlying tendencies. Paraphilia like the desire to amputate oneself or the lust for amputees is only prevalent among men. Treatment consists of antiandrogens, thus supporting an often preexisting transsexual tendency."

"Our society can live with transsexuals for the most part. With machismo and sadism anyway. But an amputee fetishist who's into stubs or empty eye sockets is certified as having a disorder, and the original conflict has to be found and removed. There is no distortion of perception there whatsoever. Self-abasement or self-empowerment through physical handicaps is more conciliatory than through blows."

"Yes, you could say that an amputee fetish is an extremely civil disorder that both demands and encourages empathy. While sadistic and masochistic tendencies are usually separate, people with a desire to be an amputee themselves frequently go for sex with amputees."

"Their tendency isn't only related to sex. They fantasize about skiing, shopping, and housecleaning with only one leg."

"Or they want to be castrated and then wouldn't be able to have sex again at all. Arm and leg amputation desires are often interpreted as a repressed desire for castration."

"Constant pathologizing robs us of so many resources."

"If people aren't permitted to irreversibly disable themselves, then one can't assume that handicapped people are also full-fledged human beings."

"There's also the idea of intellectual wholeness. But the normal would constantly have to be relativized. Bodily constitution is more obvious."

"If someone were to purposely give themselves a mental disability, he wouldn't have an easy time of it."

"It would be denied and the procedural would be emphasized. At that moment, the person was not aware that he was permanently impairing his thinking. Just as the desire for amputation can also be misunderstood as masochism."

"And what about the ones that are into sex *with* morons?"

"There's no medical term for that anyway. Not because that kind of behavior isn't pathologized, but because the possibility of it being a concrete desire is just ignored."

A handicap bus full of passengers drives up, forcing the group to step aside.

"Should we first go to the café in the park? I need to get really awake again."

"Then you'll just fall asleep in the grass. Come on, we're going in now."

"But what are we doing, saying that we're from the Sexual Deaconry? Don't we need a pretext? Like Claudia Cardinale had a pot of hot coffee when she went out to her sex-starved workers."

"It says here what they offer: electronic-waste recycling, laundry, gardening, file and data elimination, sewing."

"We're going to the laundry. Since we don't have anything to change into, we'll just undress in front of them. No one is going to restrain us. It takes a few minutes for the police to arrive."

"The handicapped people will be immediately taken away from us. Then we've achieved nothing. We only unsettled them and it goes on our records. We have to found our own organization to take care of the handicapped."

"First we would need several years of training."

"And then uptight relatives convict us of sexual abuse. No, we have to offer our services in a completely open way. The usual marketing: ads, Internet presence, interviews, talk shows…"

A group of three spazzes and two mongols is led out by attendants. When they are out of earshot Sarah says, "Let's follow them slowly."

They leisurely set themselves into motion. Repeatedly stopping to look at the flowers. On the left, in a fenced-in area of the gardening department, sheep are grazing, helping them slow the pace even more.

"Look, the attendant in the red jeans is missing two fingers on the left hand."

"And what thick socks he's wearing."

"Does that mean we're not needed?"

"Maybe it was insurance fraud."

"Don't you think we should mutilate ourselves first, so that we can better put ourselves in the handicapped people's place?"

"But that reduces our value. Handicapped people also aren't particularly into handicapped people."

"Don't we have to fight their being just as hung up on the same completion ideal as normal people?"

"Would what the already-handicapped people think in this case even matter at all? Can a revolution really be a revolution if there's no readiness to be physically victimized? And what could be more radical than to amputate something from oneself—in a society that still sanctions the death penalty more readily than punishment by the chopping off of a hand."

"It also condemns the direct infliction of pain and yet endorses masochism."

"Masochism isn't conducted in public. But we would openly show our stubs. Without the shame that the involuntary handicapped have. We would canoodle and stroke the stumps. We would paint funny faces on them and wear the little finger as an amulet—that is our 'we.'"

"The one without arms carries the one without legs."

"You can't get very far like that."

"But we also have to live from something. Robbing banks like in the RAF days isn't possible anymore. Instead we'll make a living selling our organs and from disability benefits."

"Insurance carefully checks your injuries. Maybe they get your arm or finger put back on, and you have pain your whole life."

"You could have it even if you succeed."

"And we're no masochists."

The attendants and the handicapped people have seated themselves on two park benches.

Sarah asks, "Mind if I sit here between you?"

By then she had already pushed herself between a mongol and a spazz.

Peter asked at the next bench, "And can I sit here?" and sits down just as quickly. He keeps looking joyfully from the left to the right.

Sarah holds a finger on her right hand under the spazz's nose, then under the mongol's. She slowly opens her legs. Cautiously, so that her neighbors don't suddenly shy away but instead resist the pressure.

Folding her pinky and ring fingers, Cecily holds up her hand to the eight-fingered attendant, looks at him imperiously and says: "If I were you…"

He calmly replies, "Then?"

She laughs. Chris and Dana do the same.

Cecily is the first to pull herself together again and says, "I couldn't do it any better myself. You do it exactly right."

Chris gets down on his knees and moves up between Cecily and the attendant, looks at him intensely, winks, and says very assertively, "See you later."

Dana and Cecily also wave at the sitters. The handicapped people happily return the greeting, the attendants cautiously.

Chris, Peter, and Sarah rise. The group turns back. The red slag covering the path produces dust with every step. It's hot out and smells like old iron and dry grass.

INGO NIERMANN & MARTTI KALLIALA

Drill Love

As part of a Drill Palace aimed at imposing new instinctual behaviors, the Drill Love module fosters loving everyone in a physical sense. Up until now architecture housing sexual pleasures has either concealed potentially distracting elements of the body (darkroom, glory hole) or offered an overview to make the best possible choice (cruising area, brothel display window). Instead, Drill Love facilitates random encounters of fully exposed strangers. Every visitor has to be naked, and on overcast days the sunlight is artificially enhanced.

Drill Love reveals the discrepancies between the old, ugly, weak, and disabled on the one hand, and the beautiful on the other, to enhance the latter's feelings of responsibility for the former. To arouse strong empathy, the other has to be either pretty similar or pretty different; those who seem to be just a tiny bit different are regarded as a threat or a failure. This effect is known from human replicas as the "uncanny valley" and explains why it's generally easier to feel sympathy for animals than for human strangers. Only the very famous and rich are supposed to show the same generosity toward humans as common people show toward animals. In public life the old, ugly, and disabled are not fully represented, while the mass media boasts images of perfection that make almost everyone feel aesthetically inferior. Instead, Drill Love offers a relentless picture of what human beings actually look like. It makes everyone whose beauty is above average feel special, and encourages him or her to be generous to those who are not that lucky, and to thus feel even more special. This starts right away at the lockers, which are set into the floor so that there's no way to hide. Getting undressed together is the first step to getting intimate. And at the end of the stay, exchanging lotion rubdowns and dressing each other is a hearty way to say good-bye.

Once undressed you can either stay in the dry zone with all-natural scents—a rather advanced behavior—or move straight to a hot-water curtain to clean yourself, be cleaned by others, and play by alternatively sticking your arm, head, belly, butt, breasts, or dick through the curtain. On the other side is a warm pool. Moisture in combination with heat commonly enhances sexual pleasure. Water smoothens your skin—immersed in it, you lose most of your weight and move more gently. Normally, to make water denser and to neutralize gravity completely, salt is mixed into floating tanks. But salt stings eyes and open wounds and constrains intense interactions. In this pool, sugar is added to the water, making it both denser and sweet.

The water flows counterclockwise in the pool. The weak ones are moved automatically while the fit and strong ones are challenged to swim against the whirlpool. As the weak and the strong ones move in opposite directions they bump into each other more or less randomly. If you want to rest or thoroughly interact you can stand on one of the islands in the pool or move sideways to one of its bays. If you (still) don't feel comfortable to show yourself having sex there are grottoes of different sizes. The small ones are for sex with just one partner, the bigger ones are for group sex.

SOLUTION 258

Water (with or without sugar) is not the only liquid available to dip into. A zone covered with slime makes interactions slippery and surprising. A zone with mud slows down every motion—some parts are deep enough to experience complete sinking but you can easily save yourself by leaning backward. A zone of hot steam dilutes your sweat. In addition, slime, mud, and hot steam might make you feel less exposed.

All the different zones are separated from each other by curtains of water, so that you can easily clean yourself in between. The curtains of water are thin enough to be able to vaguely see and hear through. All over the place dispensers for condoms and lubricant are set into the floor. As on modern children's playgrounds, the floor is a bit soft and bouncy.

No architecture can completely determine how it's used. A darkroom can work just as well as a place to play hide-and-seek, dine sensually, or get voluntarily robbed. Drill Love offers opportunities not just to experience pleasure and sex with strangers, but care and love. Still, it's the visitors who have to make this happen anew every day.

Drill Love Master Plan

The tentative master plan of the Drill Palace describes a series of loosely conjoined pavilions, "modules," arranged in a linear plan. Each module houses a different drill in a purpose-built structure, supporting its choreography through elementary material and spatial affordances: separation, enclosure, subdivision, letting in or omitting light, heat, moisture, (anti)gravity. It's an architecture reduced to and constructed with a handful of generic elements. Here, humans are tropical mammals again, occupying hypothetical archetypes of a new species of public space, subjected directly to the risks and opportunities this constructed environment affords.

To paraphrase Michel Foucault, a communal edifice built to house workers could just as well function as a prison or theater for unlimited sexual practices: the structure of things in itself cannot produce freedom or oppression, it requires the actual practices and exercise of freedom or oppression. That is to say, the architecture of the palace holds no illusions: to drill oneself, one must comply with the drill; to be loved, one must exercise love.

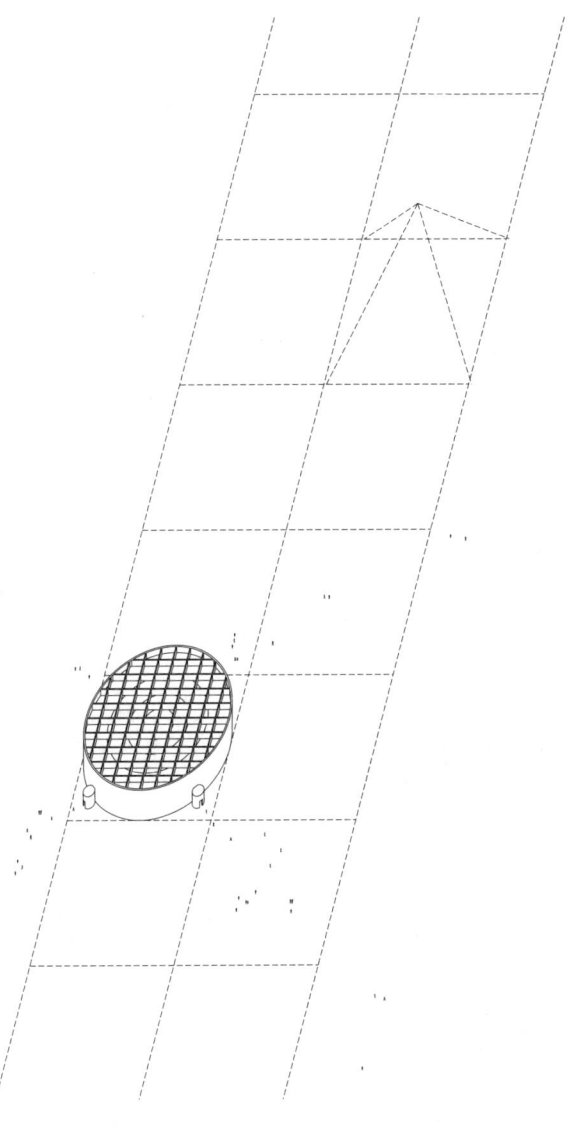

Drill Palace master plan (detail) showing Drill Love.

DRILL LOVE

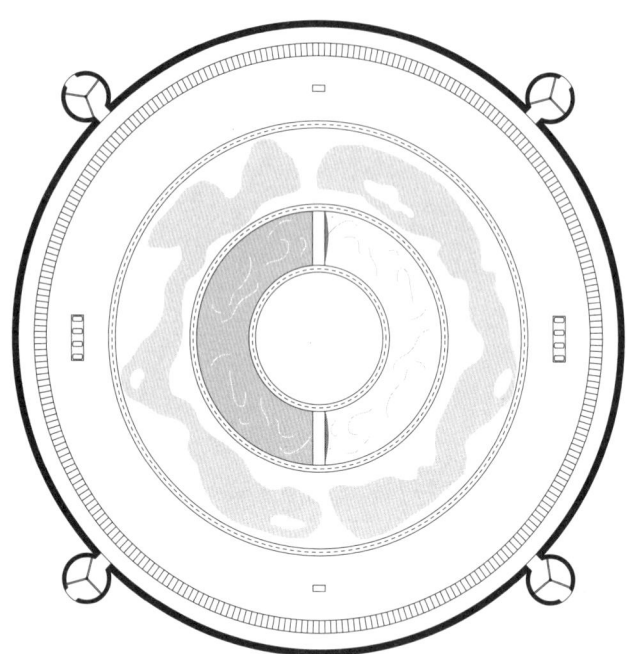

Zones, perimeter to center:
– Circulation
– Lockers
– Dry area with soft floor and toilets
– Whirlpool, islands, and grottoes
– Mud/Slime
– Steam

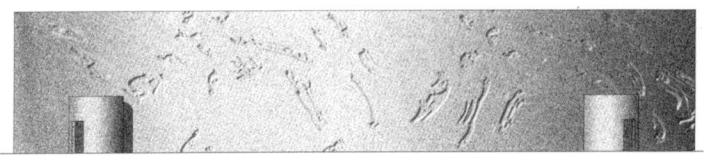

Drill Love elevation.

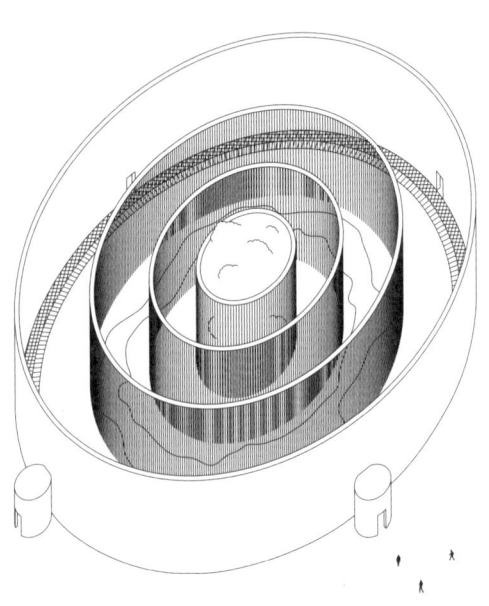

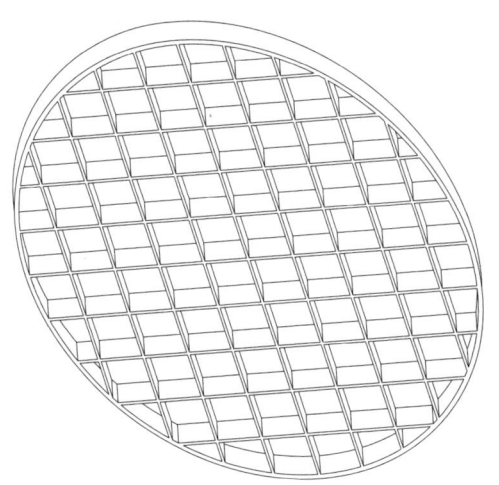

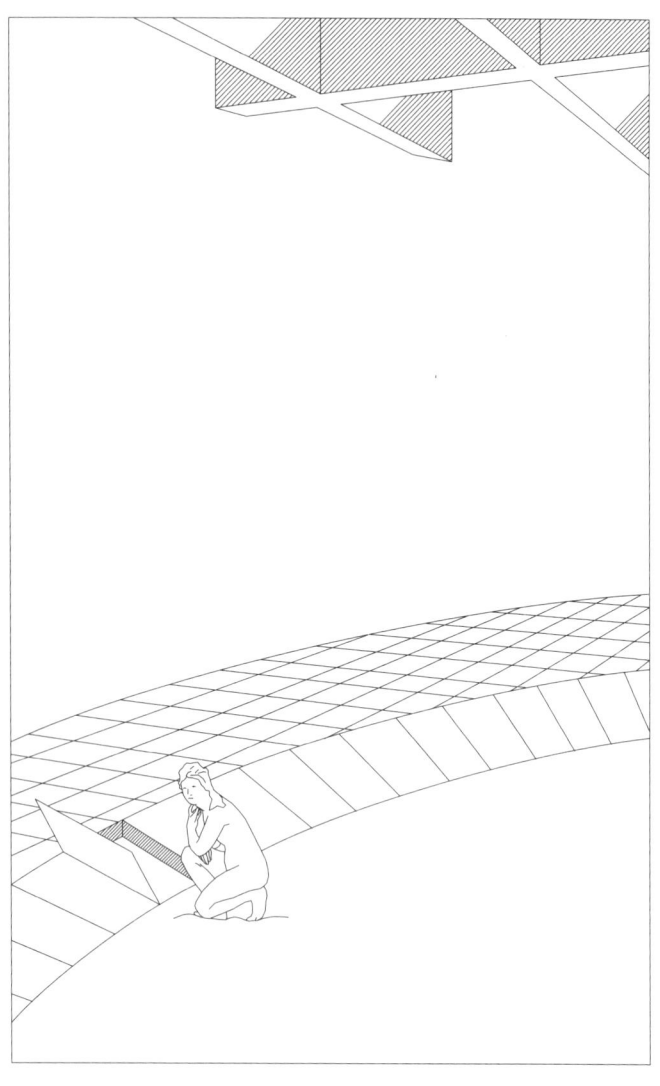

When undressing there is nowhere to hide.

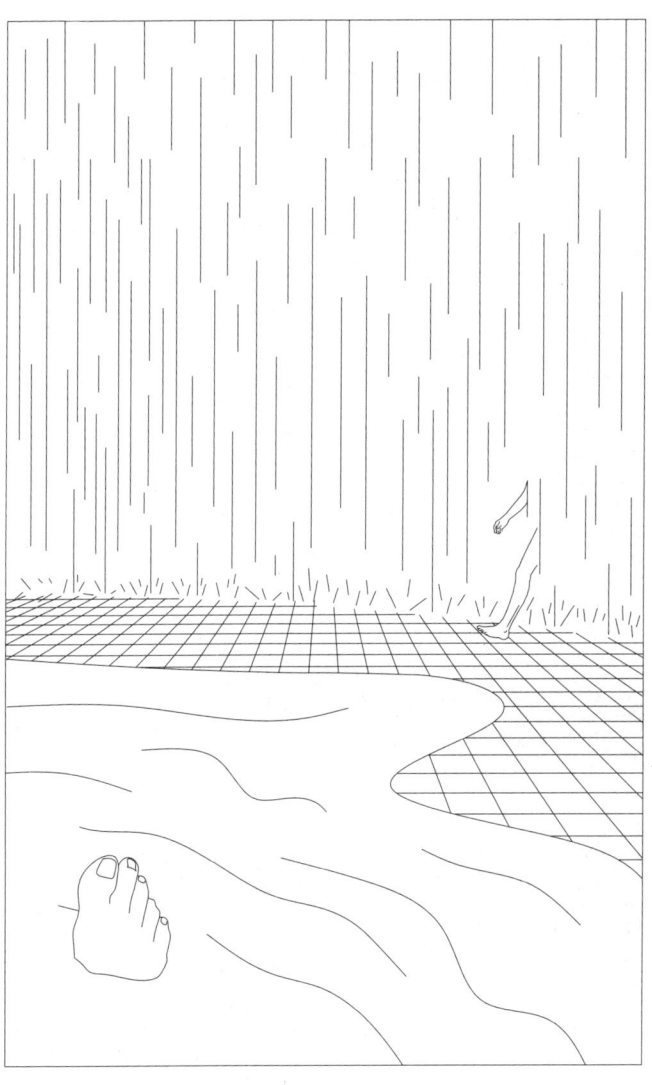

The whirlpool's sugar makes bodies float.

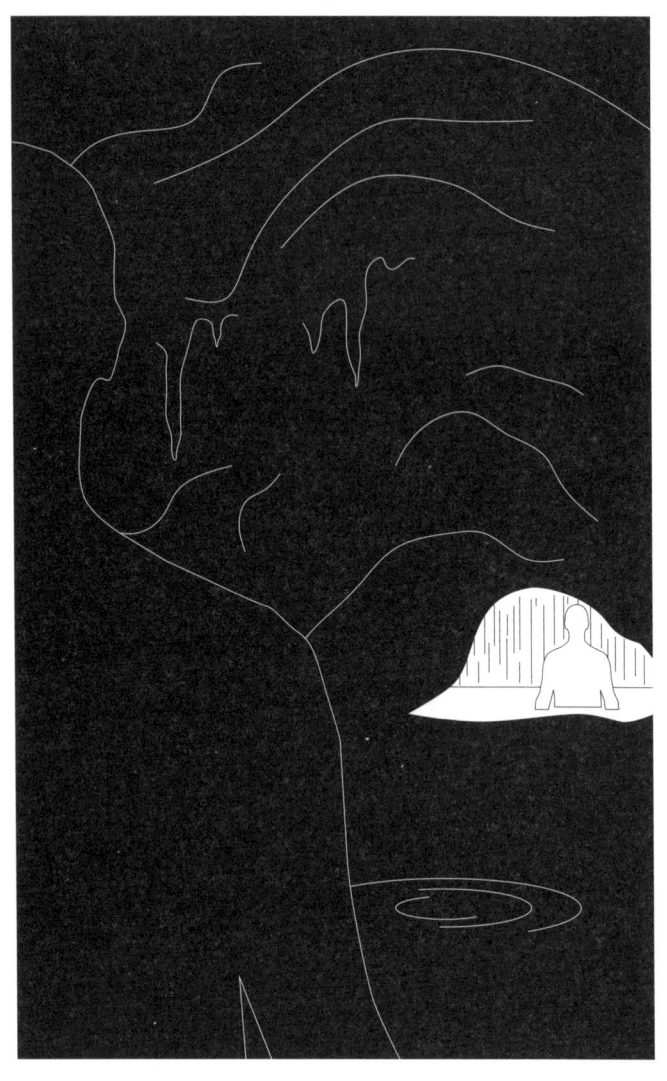

Grottoes provide a degree of privacy.

Steam blurs one's field of vision.

IGNACIO VIDAL-FOLCH

WANTED
Traveling Companion for Long Journey

We spent the afternoon, as we do every Friday, gathered round the fireplace, the wood pleasantly crackling as it gradually burned away amid the flares of traditional comfort. The fact is that if we didn't have the club, I don't know where we'd be or what we'd be doing. There's not much to do outside the club after nightfall.

There we were, as always, the usual set. The lawyer, the doctor, the chemist, and I, as well as the rentier, who had somehow attached himself to us and whose presence we had grown accustomed to despite his constant references to his dead mother, whom he called "mommy" (a loathsome habit), in remarks such as "I have never gotten over mommy's death," "As mommy used to say," and "mommy was such a marvel in the kitchen, you can't possibly imagine."

We were talking, I believe, of the ship that blew up in mid-flight the other day, killing all the crew and passengers on board, more than a thousand settlers, now bodies torn limb from limb, floating about in the ether. It was then that someone, perhaps the doctor, quoted Pascal's most famous maxim: "Tout le malheur des hommes vient d'une seule chose, qui est de ne pas savoir demeurer au repos dans un chambre."*

---

* "All of humanity's problems stem from man's inability to sit quietly in a room alone."

We savored these words for a moment, until the chemist muttered, "My guru says that one shouldn't flee from solitude but plunge into it."

"Plunge into it ... plunge into it..." I said. "These Zen Buddhist aphorisms sound fine in theory, but in practice ordinary mortals long for precisely the opposite."

"What do ordinary mortals long for?" asked the lawyer.

"To leave loneliness behind and to move on from talking to themselves to conversing with others."

"Yes, that's possible," said the rentier. "You spend the day talking to the wall and end up sick and tired."

"And those of us who can't sleep do so all night as well," said the chemist. "The inner voice is a background noise, a damned buzzing in the ears."

The rentier then remarked that his secretary, who was quite young, very good looking and a bit of a ladies' man, had asked if he could borrow some money from him. The secretary had seemingly grown weary of the disappointments he had suffered at the hands of women. Over the last twenty years, he had fallen in love, sometimes seriously, with young girls and mature matrons, with tall blondes and short brunettes, with almond-eyed Asian girls and blue-eyed Scandinavians. His romances invariably ended in heartbreak. Occasionally he grew tired of the woman; sometimes it was she who turned her attentions elsewhere.

"He's had enough of hope followed by disillusion, of looking for his soul mate and of meeting with one fiasco after another," the rentier explained. "I think he's an idealist."

"And this secretary of yours can't live on his own, like everyone else?" asked the chemist.

"No, he can't stand it. He has a great 'superfluity of love' that he wants to give. He says he needs someone to love, a receptacle into which he can pour all the love he feels. So, he's getting the money together to duplicate himself. He's asked me to help him out financially."

"What, are you going to give him money?"

The rentier shrugged his shoulders and said, "It might be useful to have two secretaries at my disposal, particularly if they owe me a favor."

We sat there, looking into the fire, watching the flames dance and pondering the secretary.

"My neighbor lives with his clone," the lawyer stated, emerging from his lethargy. "I always get them confused when I meet them in the elevator, because not only is the clone exactly like him physically, but he's had a copy of his consciousness installed in it. So they are identical. They even have the same tic—the same spasmodic blinking of the left eye."

"My cousin has done exactly the same—"

"And," the lawyer interrupted me, "they both say they are very pleased, and I can confirm they do live very happily together. They understand and are fond of each other! To see them strolling about arm in arm at dusk in the park next to the house, to see them occasionally pause amid the flowers and kiss each other on the lips, it really is a sight to behold."

"A captivating sight?"

"A disturbing sight?"

We remained unsure as to whether it was captivating or disturbing, or how people reacted to the lawyer's neighbor, walking along the paths in the park arm in arm with his clone for all the world like two lovers, because at that moment the steward came over to stoke the fire and to inquire whether we needed anything. This steward is, of course, efficient and we have no complaints. But to our minds he is not quite as agreeable as the previous one, who was naturally cordial and happy to serve, whereas this one is somewhat stiff and there is something artificial—mechanical— about him.

"My cousin has also had himself duplicated," I repeated. "But his was a special case. He had to travel to some colony or another light years away and even though he placed advertisements here, there, and everywhere, he couldn't find anyone who wanted to go with him."

"The fact of the matter is that no one can now bear the company of other people," said the lawyer. "Can you imagine what those journeys that go on for months and months must be like, shut up in a capsule with someone else? They must be hell And alone? Unbearable tedium."

It didn't seem to me appropriate to tell them that my cousin, a plainspoken, modern man not given to profound thought or sentiment, means to eject his clone when he's about to arrive at the aerodrome of his destination. (I remember my cousin when we were teenagers on Earth. He was a charming kid with a soft, singsong voice that seemed to vibrate with harmonious resonances like a human harp, but in his eyes you'd sometimes see a spark of ruthless determination.)

"I don't think," said the chemist, yawning, "that duplicating oneself is preposterous. Indeed, it even seems to me to be a sensible and reasonable solution. Who's going to understand you better than you yourself? Who could you ever love more?"

"There are people who hate themselves," the rentier objected.

"They're ill. There are treatments for that," replied the doctor.

And at the opposite extreme, the rentier wanted to know, were we not slightly shocked by those cases of men so infatuated with themselves that they had themselves replicated ten or even twelve times and lived with all these replicas in the same house as if they were back in the days of tribes or extended families?

"There are people who even have their dog or cat duplicated. I don't approve of that! What do you think?"

"Well, cats and dogs…" The chemist did not even trouble himself to finish the sentence. The rentier went on: "Would you all have yourselves duplicated?"

"Well, yes," replied the lawyer. "So long as my double was forty years younger than I am now. Because when I was that age, I was callow but I was youthful, I had plans, ideas, dreams, I was worthy of affection, passionate. In short, I was charming!"

The doctor remembered him from that era and confirmed that the lawyer had indeed been a very interesting and original young man.

"As for me, of course I would have myself duplicated," I declared. "I would love to get home and find a creature identical to myself there, but only so long as he was small. Myself in reduced size. It would be nice to arrive home in the evening and for a little guy exactly like me to come out and greet me…"

"Are you talking about a son-clone?" asked the chemist.

"No, not a son, no! I'm talking about a dwarf-clone. Children grow up and leave—how awful! No, I repeat, a dwarf. No more than four feet tall. And he should repeat everything I say, like an echo."

At this point I realized we had been joined by the engineer, who was listening, leaning on the back of the lawyer's chair. In an even voice, he interjected, "You have no idea. What kind of world are you living in? You ought to get out of the club every now and then and see what's going on in the streets. Don't you read the papers? Everyone is cloning themselves. It's an epidemic. No—to be more accurate—it's a fashion. And you," he turned to the rentier, "I advise you to keep a close eye on that secretary of yours. It's very odd that he should ask you for money when there are all kinds of offers that mean everyone can afford to duplicate themselves … But beware," he added, "all that glitters is not gold. Cases of 'domestic violence' are cropping up, copies that kill their originals and originals that murder their clones. Jealousy, apparently. It seems that in some cases there is terrible jealousy!"

"Jealousy of oneself?" objected the doctor.

"Living with someone is always difficult,"

said the lawyer, slipping back into his torpor. "I can understand why sometimes living with oneself might prove unbearable."

It was then that the steward came to revive the fire. We all took the opportunity to order more drinks and the engineer, who was in good humor after his little speech, asked him—of all the impertinence—whether he had a real heart in his chest or just a tin can.

"A tin can, sir, a tin can," said the steward, horrified. And he went off, his shoulders hunched, repeating, "A tin can, for the love of God, a tin can!"

We all laughed.

"On these enormously long journeys, who could put up with anyone?" sighed the lawyer, looking despondently at his full glass.

The engineer said, excitedly, "I myself sometimes think of duplicating myself. I would like to know what it's like to see my double wearing my clothes, to see myself cooking or looking out of the window and scratching my head, talking on the phone, laughing from time to time, and washing myself in the bathroom, and dressing and undressing myself. I don't know whether I'd like it…"

The chimney was drawing admirably and the fire was burning strongly. We were all having a good time. I looked at the faces of the doctor, the lawyer, the chemist, the rentier, and the engineer, and I wondered—I know it's ridiculous—whether they were originals or replicas. I say ridiculous because, among other things, what difference does it make?

200 WATER

You've built a respectable career in a little respected business. You've played by the rules for decades. You believe you still have a future. You've invested your money wisely in your body and your persona. You had your legs extended, but kept your breasts small and your eyes Asian. Plenty of exercise, cultural training, pricey diet. You get more lucrative contacts. They give you a 3BR. Your own. Outside company territory, on the island. You spend on decoration and the best gear: 3-D motion capture, daylight projector, invisible sensors. You squeeze six different personae into 1,300 square feet.

 Your favorite is Mademoiselle. Obviously. Best clothes, lingerie, and jewelry. Mademoiselle has the best accent and practices conversation. Never dirty. You don't mind talking dirty. You are good at it. It's all very refined. No pain or violence, they leave traces. In places you can and can't see. Mademoiselle smokes, which looks good on cam. Nobody knows that you do inhale. You never swallow, because no physical matter is exchanged. Ever. That would be a breach of contract, the end of your career, possibly your life. You play by the book. Impulses, frequencies, light waves, olfactory projections. That's how you people operate.

 Until Boris contacts you. Like all your clients he is an important asset to the company. He lives outside the territory but visits often. You think you remember him saying that he deals with waste. You know you remember his exact address: 200 Water

Street in the Financial District. You wonder why he tells you this. It looks different than any other private residence you've ever seen. It is more of a space that is defined by the outside. Glass walls. Natural light. Inside the weather. Abstract and alive. It scrapes the sky.

You see it only on camera. You take it for a warehouse and the date a misassignment. You think it's a 3-D rendering. Boris tells you the furniture are originals from some twentieth-century artist. You forget the artist's name. The bed is on a platform that floats four inches above the ground. A few wooden chairs, a table, no decoration. You think you have very little to play with. He says that is the whole point. You start to like the place.

You do not have any real-life friends. You chat with the other girls of your professional tribe but it's mostly shop. Gossip about indexed clients, new script ideas, meds, failed surgery, successful manicures, props, personal safety, and such matters. You don't unveil any secrets. It's competitive. You suspect you are the oldest around.

One day you hire a personal groomer. Yee is fired from the SoHo shop. The company reluctantly approves. They have no reason to doubt you. Yee changes your life. You have physical contact with one person on a daily basis. You are the same ethnicity, similar body. Yee listens. She only knows reality. Sometimes you let her play with your gear. She's clumsy. She says she loves it. She gives you advice. She's like a sister.

You tell her about Boris. How he has a uniform: dress shirt, the suit trousers, jacket thrown over a zigzag chair, barefoot. You can't tell if he is tall.

The place makes it difficult to gauge proportions. He always undresses during your engagement, never before. You adopt this routine. It gives you more to play with. You expand your wardrobe and the script of your engagements. They become longer in duration, and are never the same. Yee points out a change in your mood. She thinks you are in love. You shake your head. She smiles. She says you should meet with him. In person. You know it is impossible. She says it is not. You mention the risks. You mention the rumors of girls who have disappeared. She nods. You drop the subject.

Boris contacts you again. You spend a marathon session with him. You don't even undress. You talk. You laugh. When you disconnect you come forever. You know it is insane. Yee thinks it is not. You know you want to do it. She offers to give you her ID. She knows excellent forgers who got her into the territory. You tell her to drop it. You hope she won't. Boris doesn't get back to you. When he does you have a plan. You know you're monitored, but have no idea to what extent. You speak to him in French. He quotes literature. You get it. He gets it.

You can't sleep. You force yourself to eat berries. You want to smell good. Your heart races. Your physician is confused. He changes the cocktail. Your heart still races. The day comes. Yee lacquers your nipples in a deep purple. She dyes and shapes your pubes into a wild flower you've never heard of. She applies the fingerprints. You exchange QR codes.

You take a ride to the Financial District. You walk along the water. It is cold. The wind inflates your silk. The sun slices through your shades. You turn toward 200 Water. The entrance looks so much smaller than on satellite. Unassuming, unthreatening. The lobby is quiet. The black glass reflects the chandelier like an explosion. The concierge looks like a concierge. You'd expect better from an expensive building. A trap? You put your hand on the scanner and swipe your QR. He's expecting you, says the concierge who looks too much like a concierge.

The elevator's mirror shows a scared you. Your skin is transparent, your contacts a cyan hue, hair a pale peach. A few strands graze your shoulders. Yee says you look like Catherine Deneuve. Yee is fond of her. Deneuve is white. You are yellow. Yee says that's not the point. You don't know what the point is anymore. The door of the elevator opens onto the penthouse. Boris is there. He is tall, thin, and delicate. He is barefoot. The windows are real. He holds out his hand. You step out of your platforms and take his hand.

He kisses your cheek. It feels like an electric drizzle. The scent of sandalwood and burned resin. His feet kiss the floor. He leads you to the bed that seems to be floating above the floor. In the room that hovers above the city. You wish it could take off. You sit down. You don't know what to say. You feel your pulse against his hands. Lights come on in the city below. You can tell he is not looking at you.

The sun flashes before it is swallowed by the Gehry. He lies back. He doesn't let go of your hand. You lie back. Green clouds rip in the sky. This is the only place that doesn't terrorize me with meaning, he says. His voice like cellophane. You know this will be the last time you'll ever see him.

DAVID PEARCE

The Reproductive Revolution: Selection Pressure in a Post-Darwinian World

Here are three predictions about life one thousand years from now:

1. Suffering of any kind will be biologically impossible. Our descendants will lead lives of genetically preprogrammed bliss whose worst "lows" surpass today's peak experiences. A thousand years hence, the heritable "hedonic set point" of ordinary waking life will have been ratcheted upward so that everyday existence feels sublime.

2. Our genetically enhanced successors won't grow old and die, but will be effectively immortal, barring accidents that mean certain brains have to be restored from digital backup.

3. Post-humans will be innately smarter than us, not just in the narrow, autistic sense of intelligence measured by contemporary IQ tests, but in a more empathetic way. To use a nonscientific term, our descendants will be "wiser" than contemporary humans.

These are bold claims. They could of course be completely wrong: futurology doesn't have a brilliant track record. However, I'm going to argue why these three seemingly unrelated developments—super-happiness, super-longevity, and super-intelligence—are intimately linked. We are on the brink of a revolution in reproductive medicine—the coming era of designer babies, a fundamental transition in the evolution of life in the universe. Evolution will shortly cease to be "blind" and "random," as it has been for the past four billion years. Instead, intelligent agents are going to choose and design genotypes in anticipation of their likely behavioral and psychological effects. Specifically, prospective parents will increasingly choose the genetic makeup of their future children rather than playing genetic roulette. Natural selection is going to be replaced by "unnatural" selection.

But first, I want to outline a very different, bioconservative vision, perhaps best represented today by the distinguished geneticist at University College London, Steve Jones.

TWO CONTRASTING VIEWS OF FUTURE HUMAN EVOLUTION

1. Bioconservatism

"If you want to know what Utopia is like, just look around—this is it," said Jones in a 2002 Royal Society debate in Edinburgh. In a talk entitled "Is Evolution Over?," Jones says, "Things have simply stopped getting better, or worse, for our species." Jones explains how there were three components to human evolution—

natural selection, mutation, and random change. "Quite unexpectedly, we have dropped the human mutation rate because of a change in reproductive patterns. [...] In ancient times half our children would have died by the age of 20. Now, in the Western world, 98 per cent of them are surviving to 21," said Jones in an interview with *The Times*.*

The mutation rate is also slowing down. Although chemicals and radioactive pollution could cause genetic changes, one of the most important mutation triggers was advanced age in men. "Perhaps surprisingly, the age of reproduction has gone down —the mean age of male reproduction means that most conceive no children after the age of 35. Fewer older fathers means that if anything, mutation is going down."

It's worth adding that some scientists and right-wing commentators go further than Jones. They argue that because (allegedly) more intelligent people have fewer children than (allegedly) less intelligent people, the intelligence of the human species as a whole is actually going to decline. This prediction isn't borne out by the long-term increase in IQ scores over the last century, the "Flynn effect." However, believers in the so-called dysgenic fertility hypothesis counter that it is possible for genotypic IQ to decline even while phenotypic IQ rises throughout the population, at least in the short run. They explain this paradox by environmental effects such as better schooling, improved nutrition, and even television viewing.

* Julia Belluz, "Leading Geneticist Steve Jones Says Human Evolution Is Over," *The Times*, October 7, 2008.

2. Biorevolution

Human evolution is about to accelerate. Selection pressure isn't going to slacken; on the contrary, we're on the eve an era of unnatural or artificial selection—a different kind of selection pressure, but one that will be extraordinarily intense, favoring a very different set of adaptations than traits that were genetically adaptive in the ancestral environment on the African savannah.

Let's quickly review some background. The Human Genome Project was the international scientific research project that aimed to determine the sequence of chemical base pairs of our DNA: the genetic makeup of our species. Researchers identified, physically and functionally, the twenty-five thousand or so genes of the human genome. The project was formally declared 99.99 percent accurate in 2003, though in reality there are a lot of loose ends to be tied up. The full implications of our deciphered code have been scarcely glimpsed. They may take centuries to unravel.

Currently, if you want your whole genome of three-billion-odd base pairs sequenced, the price is around a few thousand dollars. In a decade or so, the cost of some estimates could be as little as ten dollars. Whatever the exact price or timing, the cost of access to one's own source code is poised to collapse. Routine access to one's personal genome will usher in an era of personalized medicine—individual drugs, dosages, and gene therapies targeted at the individual rather than the scatter-gun approach we see in clinical pharmacology (and recreational drug use) today.

Yet we're not just heading for an era of personalized medicine—we're on the eve of an era of personalized reproductive medicine: "designer babies," to use the popular term. The phrase suggests something frivolous, akin to designer clothes. But choosing the genetic makeup of your child may soon become the badge of responsible parenthood—distinct from throwing the genetic dice and hoping they roll the right way, as now. A reluctance to pass on harmful code to our children won't just apply to obvious autosomal dominant conditions, like the neurological disorder Huntington's disease. What prospective parent, if offered the choice, is deliberately going to pass on genes for hemophilia, sickle cell anemia, or muscular dystrophy? It has been estimated that on average we each carry four lethal recessive genes. In a future of post-genomic reproductive medicine, the selection pressure against, say, the cystic fibrosis allele, the cause of the most common life-limiting autosomal recessive disease among people of European heritage, is going to become intense, as indeed is selection pressure against a whole range of genes that cause or contribute to physical disease. Currently, we're used to Googling prospective partners on the Internet to find out more about them. Looking ahead, what responsible prospective parent will neglect to check their partner's DNA—and their own—before having children? This doesn't mean that anyone who wants a child will reject an asymptomatic partner who carries a recessive copy of a "nasty" gene. Instead, responsible parents can use preimplantation diagnosis and germline gene therapy to ensure that potentially harmful genes like the recessive cystic fibrosis allele aren't passed on to their children.

Genetic Roulette versus Designer Babies

Yet how about heritable psychological traits, "personality genes," that contribute to psychological pain? Not merely is there no consensus on whether some of their less pleasant variants should be classed as pathological, here too things are much more complex technically than for monogenic disorders like cystic fibrosis—there is no such thing as a single gene "for" depression or anxiety disorders or jealousy or obsessive-compulsive disorder, and so forth. But there are alleles and genotypes that predispose to depression or anxiety disorders or jealousy or obsessive-compulsive disorder—and other polygenic, multifactorial psychological conditions. So if there is a particular allele—a variant gene—that makes it, say, 5 percent more likely that a particular trait such as low mood or chronic anxiety will be expressed, or an allele that makes its bearer 5 percent more or less anxious or more or less depressive, then what percentage of prospective parents will purposely choose the less pleasant variant for their children? Yes, there are numerous complications: for instance, pleiotropy, where a single gene influences multiple phenotypic traits; alternative splicing, whereby a single gene may produce different proteins in different settings; genomic imprinting, a parent-dependent form of gene expression; non-Mendelian inheritance in the form of trans-generational epigenetic effects; and so forth. More generally, critics of the new genetic medicine worry about creating "designer personalities." Other things being equal, however, most informed parents will presumably choose the more compassionate option for their child.

Indeed, one Oxford professor of ethics goes further. Professor Julian Savulescu argues that we are morally obligated to select genetic blueprints for children with the greatest chance of leading the best life: what Savulescu dubs the "Principle of Procreative Beneficence."

This conjecture isn't premature. For example, people who inherit two copies of a "short" version of the chromosome 17 serotonin transporter gene, 5-HTTLPR, have an 80 percent chance of becoming clinically depressed if they experience three or more negative life events in five years. By contrast, genetically resilient people who inherit the long version have only a 30 percent chance of developing mental illness in similar circumstances. If offered the choice via preimplantation diagnosis, would you opt for the short or the long serotonin transporter gene variant for your future child? Or would you decline to choose, putting your faith in God or Mother Nature?

Right now, of course, this kind of scenario still sounds far-fetched. Later this century and beyond, are prospective parents really going to enroll in courses in behavioral genetics and molecular biopsychiatry before having kids? For sure, certain genetic decisions are in principle straightforward—for example, gender selection, or whether to pass on a cystic fibrosis allele. Such decisions are taken by some prospective parents in a few countries already. But other genetic decisions will be much more complicated, not least for "mood genes" that help determine a person's average level of well-being or ill-being over a lifetime.

For what it's worth, I think that taking advanced courses in behavioral genetics, or at least seeking genetic counseling, will be morally incumbent on anyone before she or he assumes the immense responsibility of having a child. But this kind of education is unlikely to be widespread in the foreseeable future. The argument presented here doesn't depend on it. Instead, in an era of mature reproductive medicine, we may forecast an abundance of user-friendly software tools to enable prospective parents to take responsible genetic decisions—distinct from blindly taking their chances in the genetic lottery of Darwinian life. For the exponential growth in computing power can be harnessed to a new growth industry of sophisticated baby-authoring software. So the average parent will no more be required to understand molecular genetics than the average contemporary Windows user is required to understand machine code. And the parallel goes further. If it's ethically acceptable to spend hours redesigning your Windows desktop the way you like it, then why not at least take a few hours to make sure that your future child is psychologically and physically healthy too?

Of course, such authoring tools open up an ethical and regulatory minefield of gargantuan proportions. Yet so does sexual reproduction: playing the genetic equivalent of Russian roulette with a child's life.

Recalibrating the Hedonic Treadmill

Prospective parents may as well choose to avoid alleles and allelic combinations associated with depression or anxiety disorders or schizophrenia when they prepare to have children. But what grounds are there for thinking that the average hedonic set point of human-kind as a whole will be ratcheted ever upward? Recall that we all have a kind of built-in hedonic treadmill that prevents most of us from remaining extremely happy or extremely miserable for very long—though of course extreme misery can seem like an eternity while it lasts. Our hedonic treadmill tends to have an approximate hedonic set point around which we fluctuate over time. This hedonic set point crudely determines the average level of subjective well-being or ill-being that most people experience throughout a lifetime. Of course we're all buffeted by external events, both pleasant and unpleasant, that affect us acutely for good or ill; but over time, we mostly revert to a (partly) heritable individual mean. In some people, the hedonic set point tends to be fixed below the Darwinian average: such people have a gloomy temperament—what the ancients would have called an excess of black bile. In other people, the hedonic set point is fixed above average: they are temperamentally optimistic. Some people's mood oscillates sharply; other people are more equable. But the current range of hedonic diversity aside, why may we predict that the typical default state of well-being of the human population is going to increase indefinitely—even after genes predisposing to anxiety disorders and clinical depression have been weeded out of the gene pool?

The plain answer is that we can't know for sure. So this is speculation. Yet here is a thought experiment. Imagine that you have the option of choosing the genetic dial settings of the hedonic set point of your future child: the degree to which he or she is temperamentally depressive or happy—or super-happy. To keep things simple, I won't yet consider the richer forms of emotional well-being, just normal hedonic tone, which we know is partly heritable. What average level of hedonic tone would you choose for your future child on a ten-point scale? (Here again I am being deliberately simplistic.) On the unscientific basis of a few straw polls conducted over the years, I'd estimate that most people if pressed would opt for a hedonic eight or nine. Yet a surprising number of respondents say ten: they would like their children to be as temperamentally happy as possible. Realistically, perhaps only a minority of prospective parents will initially want to have children disposed to be naturally super-happy by contemporary norms. But most parents will want happy children, as distinct from depressive, moody, anxiety-ridden children. Not least, happy children are more fun to raise. Happy, resilient, self-confident children are also more likely to be "successful" overachievers in the traditional Darwinian sense: we needn't suppose that prospective parents care only about the happiness of their future kids—many parents-to-be are of course highly ambitious for their offspring. Anyhow, on this argument, the average, genetically constrained set point of emotional well-being of our species is destined to rise over time as a reflection of these individual parental choices, as tomorrow's enhancement technologies shift social norms of well-being and become the next generation's remedial therapies. The depressive realism of one century may become the affective psychosis of the next. Over time, an analogous selection pressure may be exerted in favor of alleles and allelic combinations predisposing to high intelligence—and perhaps even genius and super-genius—although here any contribution to enhanced quality of life will be indirect. In any event, over a whole spectrum of physical and psychological traits, we may predict that germ-line enhancement will become germ-line remediation as the average level of biological well-being improves across human society. As biophysicist Gregory Stock notes in *Redesigning Humans*, "The arrival of safe, reliable germline technology will [...] transform the evolutionary process by drawing reproduction into a highly selective social process that is far more rapid and effective at spreading successful genes than traditional sexual competition and mate selection."* Thus the tempo of worldwide mood enrichment may accelerate.

Critically, the genetic mood-enrichment conjecture doesn't hypothesize the future existence of any megaproject to make a happier world. The possibility of such a pan-global project can't be excluded—grandiose and fanciful as the idea of some kind of hedonistic imperative now sounds. Currently only the tiny Himalayan kingdom of Bhutan officially exalts Gross National Happiness over Gross National Product. If hedonic enrichment were internationalized and pursued with scientific rigor, then the selection pressure against nastier Darwinian genotypes would be even more severe than anticipated here. Now personally, I advocate a worldwide abolitionist project laid down as official United Nations policy. Not least, only a global megaproject can ever extend the abolition of suffering to the rest of the living world. Ecosystem

* Gregory Stock, *Redesigning Humans: Choosing Our Genes, Changing Our Future* (Boston: Houghton Mifflin, 2003), 3.

redesign, cross-species depot contraception, and eventually rewriting the whole vertebrate genome can't be achieved via private initiative. However, such a megaproject isn't imminent. Less extravagantly, global mood enrichment may be the collective outcome of billions of personal reproductive decisions made by individual parents-to-be during the next century and beyond.

Phrased in the language of designer babies, the prospect of species-wide hedonic enrichment evokes sinister images—even though it promises to make the world a much happier place. Do we really want parents controlling the destiny of their future children? But we have to be careful about how we frame the issue here. Just as physical good health is empowering, and doesn't determine what you do with your life, likewise being temperamentally happy and psychologically robust doesn't determine what you actually do with your life either. Like physical health, mental health tends to empower rather than constrain. Genetically hardwired mental super-health is potentially even more empowering. It makes you psychologically indestructible. It stops you ever becoming depressed or anxiety-ridden—and suffering the crippling loss of life opportunities that such conditions entail. Moreover, in the future anybody who isn't satisfied with aspects of their core personality, and who doesn't want to use consciousness-altering drugs to change it, can practice somatic gene therapy. We won't always be at the mercy of a scrambled mix of our parents' genes as now, whether those genes have been passed on by accident or design.

FUTURE NOCICEPTION: THE END OF PHYSICAL PAIN?

So far I've discussed the abolition of suffering, and how psychological pain can be genetically eliminated over time. But what about the terrible scourge of raw physical pain? Surely, the skeptic might wonder, genes that promote pain sensitivity in response to tissue damage will be as adaptive one thousand years from now as they are today—and as they were in the ancestral environment. So the prediction that one thousand years hence, the worst experiences that anyone undergoes will be richer than today's peak experiences sounds like a pipe dream. How is this even technically possible, let alone sociologically realistic?

Well, there is a short-to-medium-term answer and a longer-term answer. Let's consider the short-to-medium-term options first.

The Cyborg Solution versus Radical Recalibration

At present there are different "natural" genetic variants that promote varying degrees of pain sensitivity—for example, variant alleles of the gene SCN9A coding for the a-subunit of the voltage-gated sodium channel Nav1.7 in nociceptive neurons; the mu-opioid receptor gene; and the gene encoding catecholamine-O-methyltransferase. Few prospective parents in the future are going to want kids who are hypersensitive to physical pain. Most parents, if given the choice, will presumably seek no more than mild to modest pain sensitivity for their offspring. Thus if genetically planned parenthood ever becomes the norm, then our pain thermostats (or "algostats," as one might call them) are likely to be genetically reset over time too.

But this recalibration doesn't actually abolish suffering, it just diminishes its prevalence and intensity when physical pain occurs. Moreover, as attested by rare cases of congenital anesthesia, children born without any capacity to suffer pain are currently liable to undergo all manner of life-threatening medical complications. So does this mean we are stuck with pain in some guise or another forever?

No, though there are formidable technical challenges to overcome. If we are to abolish physical pain altogether, I think there are two long-term options. These two options are not mutually exclusive, but I will consider them separately. Recall how silicon robots with the right functional architecture can get by fine without the nasty "raw feels" of phenomenal pain; they can be programmed to avoid and respond flexibly and adaptively to noxious stimuli. Clearly, there is a distinction between the physiological function of nociception and the subjective experience of phenomenal pain; they are dissociable even in organic robots like us, not just our inorganic counterparts. So likewise, in theory, future humans could computationally off-load everything nasty or routine onto prosthetic devices, nanobots and the like, preserving only the life-enriching forms of sentience and discarding the ugly Darwinian junk. This is what we may call the "cyborg solution." Its main advantage in the long run is that it permits maximum lifelong bliss for all sentient life. Thus its ultimate adoption would seem mandatory for a classical utilitarian ethic. But assuming that we don't go down the cyborg route, there is another option. In principle, we can radically reset the scale of the pleasure/pain axis in the mind and brain. All that is needed for an organism to respond adaptively to a changing and potentially hostile environment is informational sensitivity to fitness-relevant changes—including the binary opposition "wonderful" versus "not quite as wonderful"—regardless of the tidal range of our emotions on an absolute hedonic scale. A narrow compass of pleasure gradients can in theory play a role analogous to pain gradients in some victims of chronic pain syndrome today.

This hypothesis is counterintuitive. One might imagine that if people always feel more or less super-well—both physically and psychologically—then they won't be motivated to act circumspectly; and therefore they will tend to hurt themselves, whether physically or emotionally or both. Who could respond adaptively to the world if consumed by a perpetual whole-body orgasm? Yet this doesn't follow. As we know today, the happiest people, the keenest life lovers, tend to be the most motivated people; it's depressives who tend to be unmotivated. Yes, there are forms of happiness associated with indolence—for example, opiated bliss. But there are also forms of happiness associated with intense motivation, forward planning, and goal-directed behavior—so-called hyperdopaminergic states. Either way, our descendants, and possibly our elderly selves, will have a choice of what kinds of physical and emotional well-being they want to enjoy, and a choice of what kinds of genetic predisposition to pass on to the next generation. If you don't want to bring any more suffering into the world, then your only option right now is not to have children. In the future, however, we'll be able to have cruelty-free children with a clear conscience—on that score at least.

Gradients of Bliss?

What's true of physical pain and depression is true of other negative states of mind. Thus the prediction that life a thousand years hence will feel orders of magnitude better than now isn't a claim that post-humans will all be uniformly happy, or that future life will be perfect, whatever that might mean. Indeed one can argue that discontent is the motor of progress, and that the functional analogues of discontent are likely to endure one thousand years from now, just as the raw feels of discontent exist at present. Admittedly, it's hard to know whether fourth millennium (post-)humans will be endowed with anything even functionally resembling the same core emotions that define our lives today. The molecular signature of some kinds of emotion— for example, disgust, panic, or jealousy—might be abolished altogether, both phenomenally and function- ally, whereas genes and a regulatory code for novel life-enriching emotions may be customized and spliced into the genome. Our perceptual and cognitive architec- ture is likely to be genetically reshaped too—probably in ways beyond the contemporary human imagination. But such innovation isn't essential for an improved quality of life. The functional analogues of anxiety and depression could still persist and yet life could always be subjectively wonderful—since it's technically possible to decouple functional role from the subjective texture of unpleasant experience as we feel it now.

Critically, I'm not arguing that our descendants will enjoy uniform bliss, and certainly not that they will be manic or "blissed out," simply that their genetically constrained floor of comparative ill-being will be higher than our absolute ceiling of well-being. Continual germ-line enhancement across the generations will create a novel motivational system. Its mechanisms of emotional homeostasis will transcend the Darwinian pleasure/pain axis. Thanks to the unfolding reproductive revolution, there will be continual selection pressure in favor of the biology of a subjectively improved quality of life. Equating net value and net happiness in the manner of classical utilitarian ethics may or may not be simplistic; but acknowledgement of the connection between enhanced value and enhanced emotional well-being is common to a whole range of ethical systems, both religious and secular. Few ethical systems give no weight to emotional well-being. Thus if a piece of music sounds a thousand times more enchanting than its predecessor, or if a work of art looks a thousand times more beautiful to behold than anything physiologically possible at present, then I think the default assumption must be that such overpowering beauty is indeed a good thing—in the absence of cogent arguments to the contrary. The new germinal choice technologies allow the creation of subjectively valuable experience on a truly prodigious scale. So other things being equal, we should embrace their use.

Spiritual Well-Being?

The approach I've sketched so far probably sounds crudely reductionist. But one needn't interpret super--happiness in just a narrow one-dimensional sense.

Take, for example, spirituality and spiritual well-being. In the future, if you are very spiritual and want to have hyper-spiritual children, then you can opt to over- or underexpress the relevant genes or allelic combinations promoting a spiritual temperament; and perhaps ultimately design angelic "spiritual" genomes for your children. Indeed if you want to be naturally super-spiritual yourself and don't want to take entheogenic drugs, then you could use autosomal gene enhancement and add extra copies or overexpress variants of alleles and allelic combinations associated with spirituality. Secular rationalists, on the other hand, may prefer to lay the genetic foundations of a worldlier well-being.

To take another example of multidimensional well-being, prospective parents may be able to choose genes and genotypes associated not just with intelligence in the simple-minded conventional sense, but with an increased capacity for empathy, involving functionally amplified mirror neurons and enhanced social cognition. Prospective parents will have the opportunity to endow their kids with an enriched oxytocin system, leading to greater trust, generosity of spirit and pro-social behavior, potentially with immense benefits for society as a whole. Such scenarios are of course speculative.

A REPRODUCTIVE ELITE?

An obvious question arises: Won't these new reproductive technologies be solely for the rich, or at least mainly for members of the prosperous developed nations who can buy the best genes, undercutting the argument from selection pressure advanced here?

Initially, surely yes. But not for long, even assuming (implausibly) that the world's poorest nations will remain poor indefinitely. Consider how rapidly Web-enabled cell phones have spread through even impoverished sub-Saharan Africa. If personal genome sequencing always costs anything like the five thousand dollars or so it does now, then only an elite of affluent Westerners could benefit from such break-throughs. If personal genome sequencing cost ten dollars or less, then effectively everyone can have it. The nature of information and information technology entails that IT-based services don't involve the consumption of scarce natural resources in the way material goods do, where one person's gain is frequently another person's loss. Only a handful of people in the world can ever own a Rolls Royce or a Maserati, and even fewer can own an original Picasso or an Old Master; but an unlimited number of people can listen to the world's entire catalogue of music, enjoy access to all its electronic games, its computer software, its movies, or indeed the whole Library of Congress. Information is effectively free, or at least it will be soon. Later this century, reproductive technologies like preimplantation genetic screening and diagnosis—techniques used to identify genetic defects in embryos created through in vitro fertilization before pregnancy—are going to become dirt cheap too. Already crude personal genotyping services are available for a few hundred dollars.

Of course it's easy to sing a happy tune with the word "soon." I'm glossing over a host of problems in the transitional era between old-fashioned sexual reproduction and true planned parenthood—"soon" in this context may mean decades, and perhaps centuries. But even on the most conservative timescales, we're on the brink of a major discontinuity in the four-billion-year odyssey of the evolution of life on Earth.

SOME UNKNOWNS
Human Cloning

One big unknown affecting any conjectures about future selection pressure is the role of human cloning. Whether human reproductive cloning takes another five years or fifty years, it's going to happen. What's less clear is the cost and expertise involved when the technology matures, and what its global implications are for selection pressure. If human cloning will always take a large team of research professionals, complex medical equipment, many failed attempts, and a great deal of money, then it will presumably always be rare. But if it can ever be done cheaply and safely at home, perhaps via DIY cloning kits available for purchase over the Internet, then human cloning could become a common way to make babies, regardless of official laws and regulations.

For the sake of argument, let's suppose that human cloning does eventually become a common mode of reproduction. It's not clear if this is a bad development per se, any more than identical twins or triplets are intrinsically bad. Either way, this possibility might seem to throw a big spanner into the argument from selection pressure I'm making here, since genetically identical babies are likely to suffer from the same problems as their father or mother if exposed to a similar environment.

Yet it seems a reasonable assumption that most future human cloners won't seek to create exact genetic duplicates of themselves, but will instead aspire to have offspring free of defects or unwanted characteristics possessed by their parent. To use a trivial example, a human cloner with thinning hair wouldn't necessarily want to have a cloned child with a predisposition to grow bald. Granted, most people who want a clone would most likely want to have children that bear a facial resemblance, but presumably carriers of the cystic fibrosis allele won't seek to pass the defective gene on to their cloned offspring. Likewise, depressive people who might like to clone themselves for the most part aren't likely to want depressive children. Cases of "negative enhancement," akin to the existing use of preimplantation genetic diagnosis to select an embryo for the presence of a particular disability such as deafness shared by one or both parents, will presumably be uncommon. So yes, if human cloning becomes widespread, and certainly if human cloning becomes cheap and ubiquitous, then its spread makes the argument from selection pressure defended here more complex; but the practice wouldn't fundamentally undercut its conclusion.

Autosomal Gene Therapy and Enhancement

Another unknown that adds to the complexity of the selection-pressure argument is the future extent of autosomal gene therapy. I've been focusing on reproduction and germ-line gene therapy and genetic enhancement; but somatic gene therapy is sure to become available and probably extensively used too. After all, if offered the choice of either taking a drug to remedy some physical or psychological defect for the rest of your life or curing that deficit with a one-off course of gene therapy, which would you choose—if you were sure that the gene therapy was safe and effective? The same is true of future enhancement technologies—though remediation versus enhancement is a naive dichotomy.

POTENTIAL PITFALLS
The Specter of Coercive Eugenics

Anyone uncritically enthusiastic about the reproductive revolution in prospect would do well to reflect on the history of the twentieth century. In the words of bioethicist Nicholas Agar, "Those who do not learn from the history of human enhancement may be doomed to repeat it." One recalls the forced segregation, sterilization, racial hygiene, the euthanasia program, and ultimately the genocide practiced in the pseudoscientific name of eugenics. Might the impending reproductive revolution lead to similar horrors? After all, there are still plenty of people in the world convinced that some races are intellectually or morally superior to other races. Might history repeat itself?

The short answer is yes, though I think such scenarios are unlikely. For a start, the totalitarian dictatorships of the twentieth century, not least the Nazi regime, all depended on censorship and a state monopoly of information. The Internet makes the creation of totalitarian dictatorships much harder; as has been well said, the Internet interprets censorship as damage and reroutes it. However, this is obviously a huge topic. To put it shortly: there is a fundamental difference between a regulatory system where eugenics (under whatever name) is practiced for the well-being of the individual—whether human or nonhuman—and an authoritarian society where eugenics is practiced for the notional benefit of a class, race, or nation.

Even so, there are clearly lots of problems with so-called liberal eugenics. For instance, there are pitfalls with prospective parents choosing enhancements that offer a merely positional advantage to their children. To give a concrete example, if parents pick genes likely to allow their child to grow taller than the current average, then there is no net benefit to either the child or society if most other parents do the same. Indeed if human stature were to become significantly higher than today, then we would all be prone to multiple health difficulties under Earth's gravitational regime. Even enhancements such as genes that may contribute to superior intelligence that sound as though they could confer intrinsic benefit—overexpressing or adding extra copies of the NRP2 or ASPM or microcephalin gene, to use a contentious, intelligence-boosting example—might arguably amount to positional goods like height. Thus women tend to find intelligence sexy in prospective mates; but presumably what's advantageous to the brainy male bearer in terms of enhanced sex appeal is relative—and not absolute—intelligence. A counter to this argument might be that there are inherent benefits to high male intelligence aside from attracting women.

In contrast with interventions that confer positional advantage, genetic enhancements that enrich subjective well-being—crudely, whether you are temperamentally happy or super-happy—would be intrinsically beneficial; they can potentially benefit everyone, regardless of where one falls on any comparative scale of well-being. Indeed technologies that biologically enrich emotional well-being are arguably the only enhancements that are intrinsically good as distinct from positionally or instrumentally good. This claim is obviously controversial; it would be contested by many bioethicists who aren't classical utilitarians.

OTHER PITFALLS?

Although designer genomes can in principle lead to vastly greater diversity, might designer genomes lead in practice to greater genetic uniformity if most parents strive to have similar kinds of "ideal" children, the supernormal reflections of preferences adaptive in our Darwinian past? Admittedly, some kinds of genetic uniformity are presumably desirable. Thus by common consent it would be a blessing if there were no gene for Huntington's disease. But twentieth-century eugenicists didn't take account of phenomena such as heterozygote advantage—normally defined as cases where the heterozygote genotype has a higher relative fitness than either the homozygote-dominant or homozygote-recessive genotype. Heterozygote advantage explains why some kinds of genetic variability persist, most famously the gene for sickle cell anemia. Analogous heterozygote advantage may exist for psychological traits too, though this is unproven.

Whatever their evolutionary origin, here are three examples where the issues are complicated.

1. The Future of Homosexuality
Even if you have absolutely no prejudices at all about

homosexuality, would you choose so-called gay genes for your child—variant alleles that predispose your child to be gay? Now of course it's possible that 50 or 150 years time, homophobia will have been relegated to the dustbin of history where it belongs; but I wouldn't count on it. In the meantime, what percentage of prospective parents, whether straight or gay or bisexual, will deliberately choose to have a gay child knowing the greater social problems that child would be likely to encounter in life due to social prejudice? If this is the case, and if there is indeed a reproductive revolution as outlined here, then it is quite likely that genes predisposing to homosexuality and possibly even bisexuality will be strongly selected against. They may even die out. If one looks in human history from classical antiquity to the present at the contribution made by people whom we would probably classify as gay or bisexual, and likewise at the contribution of their close genetic relatives, then this is not an outcome to be contemplated lightly. On the other hand, it's also possible that many gay couples will use the new reproductive technologies to have gay children, rendering the gay-extinction scenario moot.

2. The Future of Bipolar Disorder

Chronic unipolar depression may be an unmitigated evil; but what about bipolar disorder, formerly known as manic depression? Bipolar disorder can undoubtedly cause terrible suffering both to its victims and their families. Yet many creative high achievers in art, science, and politics have at the very least been soft bipolars. Is there a danger that something valuable will be lost if in the future prospective parents weed out

THE REPRODUCTIVE REVOLUTION

of the gene pool alleles associated with bipolarity? Again, this is a huge topic.

3. The Future of Autism Spectrum Disorders

Classical autism is characterized by varying degrees of "mindblindness" and deficits in social interaction; deficits in language, communication, and the capacity for social play; and multiple stereotypies of behavior. The three most common forms of autism spectrum disorders are classical autism, pervasive developmental disorder not otherwise specified, and Asperger's syndrome. Whereas children with, say, Down syndrome or Williams syndrome can be abnormally sociable—and therefore rewarding to raise—by contrast autistic children with an absent or underdeveloped theory of mind commonly cause great distress to their caregivers. It is hard to bond with someone who always treats you as an object. Thus any genetic disposition to autism might seem a prime candidate for elimination from the gene pool as the reproductive revolution gathers pace. However, some of the greatest scientists who ever lived, notably Isaac Newton, Albert Einstein, and Paul Dirac, fulfill many or all of the diagnostic criteria for Asperger's syndrome. To what extent was their scientific acumen separable from their pathologies of mind?

CALCULATING RISK/REWARD RATIOS

If there are likely to be so many possible adverse or unintended consequences, or both, of the new reproductive medicine—and perhaps dystopian outcomes no one has even considered—then why forge ahead? Why not outlaw the new reproductive technologies altogether, or at least drastically restrict their use to simple Mendelian genetic diseases of the body rather than complex disorders of the mind and brain? After all, there is no way we can computationally model all the ramifications of even modest rewrites of the human genome.

Here the question comes down to an analysis of risk/reward ratios—and our basic ethical values, themselves shaped by our evolutionary past. Lest extensions of the new reproductive medicine seem too rashly experimental even to contemplate, it's worth recalling that each act of old-fashioned sexual reproduction is itself an untested genetic experiment, the outcome of random mutations and meiotic shuffling of the genetic deck, and with no happy ending to date. So just who are we to accuse of reckless gambling? As it stands, all of us are genetically predestined to grow old and die; and in the course of a lifetime, the great majority of humans will experience periods of intense psychological distress—for instance, loneliness and heartache after an unhappy love affair. Our social primate biology ensures that most of us sometimes experience, to a greater or lesser degree, all manner of nasty states that were genetically adaptive in the ancestral environment—jealousy, resentment, anger, and so forth. Hundreds of millions of people in the world today suffer bouts of depression; others live with chronic anxiety. One might say these phenotypes are part of "what it means to be human." Worse, we pass a heritable predisposition to these horrible states on to our children.

Bioconservatives, religious traditionalists, and social reformers alike would contest this bleak analysis.

If you believe that human life today is fundamentally good, and viciously unpleasant states of mind are an aberration that can be mostly remedied by improving society, then you will need compelling reasons before wanting to change the regime of ordinary sexual reproduction as it exists now. Most likely, you will be loathe to support anything like the reproductive revolution predicted here, and focus entirely on its potential dangers. The specter of *Brave New World* will probably loom large in any discussion. If, on the other hand, you think that Darwinian life is cruel and tragic by its very nature, then you are more likely to be willing to contemplate radical alternatives to the genetic status quo, despite the possible risks.

My own view of the risks and uncertainties is that there is a critical distinction between trying to abolish suffering exclusively via social reform and abolishing suffering directly via biotechnology. As we know, utopian social experiments typically go wrong, sometimes hideously wrong, and end up causing a lot of suffering instead. The abolitionist project of eradicating the biological substrates of suffering sounds like just another utopian scheme, whether it's touted as a grandiose species project or simply as a byproduct of the reproductive revolution explored here. Although the abolition of psychological pain is arguably no more utopian in principle than pain-free surgery, it could presumably go wrong in unanticipated ways too. Perhaps we'll unwittingly create a fool's paradise. But if and when we ever abolish the molecular underpinning of unpleasant experience, and it becomes physiologically impossible for any sentient being to suffer, we thereby change the very meaning of what it is for anything to "go wrong." Unwelcome surprises where no one gets hurt are very different from unwelcome surprises where they do. For what it's worth, I think the abolition of involuntary suffering is the precondition of any civilized post-human society; and therefore a risk worth taking.

THE END OF SEXUAL REPRODUCTION?

I've outlined grounds for believing that our nastier Darwinian emotions will be selected against in future. Yet there is a fundamental objection to the argument from selection pressure that I've sketched so far. Surely most people, not least teenagers, will carry on producing babies by having sex together regardless of any so-called reproductive revolution of laboratory-mediated conception. Unplanned pregnancies are extremely common even in an age where contraceptives are widely available. Yes, maybe responsible, forward-looking parents will seek to ensure that they have children who are free of genetic handicaps, who are joyful, ultra-intelligent, super-empathetic and psychologically robust. And maybe in the future such responsible parents-to-be will practice preimplantation genetic diagnosis, use germ-line gene therapy, and pursue some of the futuristic interventions described here. But that won't stop feckless teenagers having unplanned babies. In addition, billions of people may be reluctant to embrace the new reproductive technologies for traditional moral or religious reasons, or simply out of custom and habit. It stretches the imagination to envisage genetically planned parenthood ever becoming as prevalent as, say, anesthetics to guarantee pain-free surgery. If most fertile women continue to bear genetically unenriched babies by the conventional route, then surely our built-in genetic tendency to all forms of Darwinian suffering is going to express itself indefinitely?

Maybe so. It's a powerful argument. Yet there are strong grounds for thinking that traditional sexual reproduction can't continue for more than a few generations. The reason is bound up with the coming revolution in antiaging medicine.

Throughout most of human history, radical life extension, let alone the prospect of eternal youth, has been the province of quacks and charlatans. To some extent it still is: swallowing a bunch of vitamin pills each day isn't going to let you live forever. But over the next few centuries, and possibly before, aging and the genes that promote or allow senescence are going to be phased out. This is of course a bold claim that I won't even attempt to defend in detail here. If you are skeptical and haven't read it already, I'd recommend Aubrey de Grey's 2007 book *Ending Aging: The Rejuvenation Breakthroughs That Could Reverse Human Aging in Our Lifetime.* Now, I am more pessimistic than de Grey about timescales. Yet the genetic and pharmacological interventions that we are already trying in nonhuman animals will eventually be tried in the human animal too. One hesitates to embrace what sounds like a facile technological determinism; but I think we can say, quite dogmatically, that if and when radical antiaging technologies become available, then the overwhelming majority of people will use them—regardless of any rationalizations of death and aging we express now. Moreover, most people will also want such treatments for their family pets; the antiaging revolution won't be confined to one species.

Let's assume for the sake of argument that there will be both a reproductive revolution and an antiaging revolution. If post-genomic medicine dramatically extends lifespan, and fewer and fewer people die of the traditional diseases of old age, then our planet will soon reach its carrying capacity. Looking centuries ahead, a rapidly expanding population of eternally youthful quasi-immortals means that human reproduction of any kind will have to become rare, and eventually a momentous event, and tightly controlled in every respect. It's here that I foresee both the greatest ethical dilemmas arising from the reproductive revolution and also the intimate link between super-happiness, super-intelligence, and super-longevity.

SELECTION PRESSURE IN AN AGE OF QUASI-IMMORTALITY

When Earth reaches its carrying capacity—the maximum packing density of sentient beings consistent with sustainable life—there will have to be immensely greater centralized control of the human reproductive system on pain of complete Malthusian catastrophe. This does indeed sound a truly sinister prediction. Perhaps one can imagine the existence of a mandatory regime of depot contraception from an early age. Yet could depot contraception really be made fail-safe? How would such fertility control be enforced? Moreover, the problem isn't just preventing reproductive accidents. The urge to have one's "own" children can be extraordinarily strong, as attested by the anguish caused by involuntary childlessness today; for many childless couples, this yearning could eclipse any general worries about the carrying capacity of the planet. A majority of people will want both to stay forever young and to have children. If radical antiaging technologies are indeed widely adopted, then a central and unavoidably intrusive control of human reproduction may be inevitable, though one may trust such powers will be accountable to democratic control. In an era of mass super-longevity, every intellectually competent citizen will presumably recognize, in the abstract, that unlimited free reproduction is physically impossible. On the other hand, some people will presumably try to have unregulated, unsanctioned children, just as they do in the People's Republic of China today, albeit without the promise of eternal youth. This is not an attractive parallel. Of course there are other social perils associated with mass super-longevity: in an era of genetically preprogrammed eternal youth, the ruling power elites may prove almost immovable in the absence of adequate democratic safeguards. But the potential loss of bodily autonomy and procreative liberty is especially troubling to the liberal conscience—and to any libertarian life extensionist.

A counterargument here is that the urge to bear children is under genetic control; and that urge will itself be amenable to biological intervention. Manipulation of our first-order desires is likely to prove biologically easier than defeating aging. Yet if most of one's enhanced fellow citizens do act responsibly and forgo or postpone reproduction, then any predisposition to "cheat" and have children might be highly (genetically) adaptive, at least in the short run. Such an outcome would be disastrous in an already overpopulated global megalopolis. Plausible group-selectionist scenarios aren't easy to construct even for the far future; hence the price of post-human super-longevity is the likelihood of ever-greater state intervention in the (hitherto) private realm—although such intrusiveness need not be subjectively distressing in any sense we would recognize today, since the functional analogue of distress might suffice. Long before any era of post-genomic medicine, Plato believed that human reproduction should be monitored and controlled by the state, a portent of totalitarian societies to come. But once we transcend the biology of human mortality, some sort of collective control of reproductive decision making may prove inescapable, even in a liberal democracy. The only alternative to such control would be draconian, state-enforced rationing of antiaging therapies: a scarcely credible reenactment of *Logan's Run*. It's important to note that this argument doesn't turn on whether it transpires that the ultimate carrying capacity of our planet is 15 billion or 150 billion or conceivably even higher packing densities. Yes, we can colonize the solar system; in theory, too, in some era of the distant future, the authorities on Earth could tell anyone who wants to have a child that they must do so on one of the colonized extrasolar planetary systems. But for the next few centuries at least, and possibly millennia, the prospect of some kind of galactic adaptive radiation is pure science fiction.

For it is hard to overstate the technical obstacles to mass interstellar travel. Quite possibly, post-humans will go to the stars, and perhaps even colonize our local galactic super-cluster in a few million years or so. Realistically, this doesn't solve the near-term demographic challenge of a massively overcrowded Earth.

Admittedly I am making a number of contestable assumptions here. I will note just three.

1. Intelligent life won't wipe itself out altogether in the next few decades. Doomsday scenarios are conceivable, but they are much harder to construct once self-sustaining colonies are established on other planets later this century.

2. There is a unique past and a unique future. This simplifying assumption is inconsistent with quantum cosmology and most likely false. However, consideration of the "branch density" measure of alternative, classically inequivalent histories in post-Everett quantum mechanics would take us too far afield in this paper.

3. Unlike futurists who believe in "uploading," I am assuming that our (post-)human descendants will retain an organic substrate—maybe augmented by Web-enabled neurochips, nanobots, bionic implants, and the like—and hence that humans won't scan, digitize, and upload themselves to dwell in another computational medium where the constraints of the Earth's ecosystem don't apply. There is no evidence that your computer is any more conscious than

an abacus, despite its greater processing power. And if a souped-up version of your computer contained a digitized representation of you, this would doubtless facilitate restoration from backups, but there are no grounds for thinking such lines of code would be conscious either—let alone "you." Yes, artificial intelligence will hasten the reproductive revolution; perhaps one day we will all become Web-enabled cyborgs. And who knows what kinds of exotic post-biological artificial life can be evolved if and when our descendants run mature quantum computers. Yet there is simply no evidence that inorganic systems with a classical von Neumann architecture support raw feels or intrinsically matter: the notion that our species might destructively upload ourselves from basement reality into digital nirvana is unworkable. So here at least I am being tamely bioconservative in assuming that Earth, one thousand years hence, will support a densely populated primordial "meatworld" of our flesh-and-blood post-human descendants.

Anyhow, to summarize, assume that the creation of new quasi-immortal beings will indeed become exceedingly rare later this millennium. Earth will be (almost) literally full. I'd argue that on such historic occasions as the creation of a new post-human being, it is unlikely that super-happy, super-intelligent agents will create the genetic malware for unpleasant, stupid, senile substrates of consciousness—for instance, archaic *Homo sapiens*. Our post-human descendants are more likely to create fellow "smart angels" instead.

The triumph of the reproductive revolution will have reshaped the post-Darwinian fitness landscape beyond all recognition—hence my (tentative) prediction that the biology of suffering and senescence is destined to pass into evolutionary history.

Etel Adnan, *1925, is a Lebanese-American poet, essayist, and visual artist. Her recent publications include *In/somnia* (2003), *In the Heart of the Heart of Another Country* (2005), *Seasons* (2008), and *Master of the Eclipse* (2009).

Douglas Coupland, *1961, is a Canadian novelist. He has published thirteen novels, two collections of short stories, seven nonfiction books, and a number of dramatic works and screenplays for film and television.

Eva Illouz, *1961, is a professor of sociology at the Hebrew University of Jerusalem. Her recent books include *Cold Intimacies: The Making of Emotional Capitalism* (2007), *Saving the Modern Soul: Therapy, Emotions, and the Culture of Self-Help* (2008), and *Why Love Hurts: A Sociological Explanation* (2012).

Martti Kalliala, *1980, is a Finnish architect currently based in Helsinki. He is the founder of the design and research practice Pro Toto and the author of the Solution series volume *Finland: The Welfare Game* (2011) with Jenna Sutela and Tuomas Toivonen.

Ben Marcus, *1967, is an American author of four books of fiction: *The Age of Wire and String* (1995), *Notable American Women* (2002), *The Father Costume*, with art by Matthew Ritchie (2002), and *The Flame Alphabet* (2012). He is an associate professor of writing at Columbia University School of the Arts, and he lives in New York and Brooklin, Maine.

Chus Martínez, *1972, is the chief curator of El Museo del Barrio in New York. Previously, she was head of department of dOCUMENTA(13) in Kassel, chief curator of Museu d'Art Contemporani de Barcelona, director of the Frankfurter Kunstverein, and artistic director of Sala Rekalde in Bilbao.

Momus, *1960, is the artist name of Nicholas Currie. He was born in Scotland and is currently living in Osaka. He has released twenty-five music albums as well as published *The Book of Jokes* (2009) and two volumes in the Solution series, *The Book of Scotlands* (2009) and *The Book of Japans* (2011).

Eva Munz, *1968, is a German writer, filmmaker, and coauthor of *The Ministry of Truth: Kim Jong Il's North Korea* (2007). She lives in New York.

Ingo Niermann, *1969, is a German novelist and editor of the Solution series. His recent publications include *Choose Drill* (2011), and—in collaboration with Erik Niedling—*The Future of Art: A Manual* (2011) and *The Future of Art: A Diary* (2012).

David Pearce is a British utilitarian philosopher, vegan activist, and cofounder with Nick Bostrom of the World Transhumanist Association (now Humanity+). He is author of "The Hedonistic Imperative" (1995), a manifesto calling for the use of biotechnology to abolish suffering throughout the living world.

Beatriz Preciado, *1970, is a Spanish philosopher and one of the leading thinkers in the study of gender and sexuality. Preciado's books include *Manifeste contra-sexual* (2000) and *Pornotopía: Arquitectura y sexualidad en "Playboy" durante la guerra fría* (2010).

Emily Segal, *1988, is a writer and artist in New York. She is a cofounder of the trend forecasting report K-HOLE and a strategist at the branding firm Wolff Olins.

Alexander Tarakhovsky, *1955, was born and grew up in the former Soviet Union and is currently a professor and laboratory head at the Rockefeller University in New York. His main field of research is epigenetics, a branch of biological science that studies the mechanism of induction and propagation of newly acquired features.

Ignacio Vidal-Folch, *1956, a writer, was born in Barcelona and lives … in Barcelona. He tried to … but, oh well, that's life!

CREDITS

"Preface: The Imperative to Love" by Ingo Niermann was translated from German by Gerrit Jackson.

"How Bondage Solves the Problem of Modern Love" by Eva Illouz first appeared on *Spiegel Online*, July 13, 2012.

"The Contra-Sexual Manifesto" by Beatriz Preciado is an excerpt from the manifesto of the same name, first published in French in 2000.

"The Completists" by Ingo Niermann was translated from German by Amy Patton and commissioned by Contemporary Fine Arts for the 2006 group exhibition "Once Upon a Time in the West."

"WANTED: Traveling Companion for Long Journey" by Ignacio Vidal-Folch was translated from Spanish by Sue Brownbridge.

"The Reproductive Revolution: Selection Pressure in a Post-Darwinian World" by David Pearce is based on a talk given at the Touch Me Festival in Zagreb in 2008.

COLOPHON

Solution 247-261: Love is part of the Solution series edited by Ingo Niermann and designed by Zak Group.

ISBN 978-3-943365-78-8

Series and book editor: Ingo Niermann
Managing editor: Max Bach

Design: Zak Group
Cover illustration: Jonas Voegeli

Printed and bound by BUD Potsdam

Sternberg Press
Caroline Schneider
Karl-Marx-Allee 78
D-10243 Berlin
www.sternberg-press.com